CHURCH IN

THE MAKING

BEN ARMENT

PUBLISHING GROUP

Nashville, Tennessee

978-0-8054-6473-3

Published by B&H Publishing Group
Nashville, Tennessee

Published in association with Yates & Yates,
www.yates2.com.

Dewey Decimal Classification: 254.1
Subject Heading: CHURCH PLANTING \ CHURCH
GROWTH \ EVANGELISTIC WORK

1 2 3 4 5 6 7 8 9 10 • 14 13 12 11 10

CONTENTS

Part 3: Deep Roots

FOREWORD

Red Rover is an interesting idea.

School kids would stand in two lines facing each other and take turns yelling out, "Red Rover, Red Rover, send Joey right over!" Then Joey would have to leave his line and run as fast and hard as he could to break through the other line of kids holding hands. If successful, he would take one member from the other team back with him to his line. If unsuccessful, Joey had to remain in the opposing team's line and then another child would be called to come over.

The game has seemed to lose some steam in the last few years. Maybe because "cooler" games developed. Maybe due to the number of kids with neck injuries from nearly being strangled trying to break through. Whatever the case, it seems for the most part that Red Rover has gone to the playground cemetery along with King of the Hill. We could hope for a resurrection.

It has occurred to me that we often try to adopt a Red Rover strategy in church planting. Like Paul in Acts 16, we hear the call, "Come over and help us!" and we react with a violent attempt to just break through the line. We have a dream in our heart to plant a church, and we become so consumed with this vision that we barrel right into a new town looking for the weakest link in the chain before ever getting an honest and clear picture of the people that live there. We start plowing into a community with strategy, plans, and really great books written by "cool" church leaders without ever considering the group of people into which we're being sent. And before we know it, we find ourselves strangled, trying to break into a community that is not ready or able to receive the church we have planned.

So let me say this: before planting a church, it's vital that we have a vision of the people to whom God has sent us. This was the crucial step that happened in Acts 16 and is inherent to the process proposed in this important church planting book. Know what God is doing among the people of the community where you have been called. Then plant a church.

In Acts 16 Paul and his companions set out to minister to people, but they ran up against barriers along the way. The Bible says in verses 6–9, "Paul and his companions traveled throughout the region of Phrygia and Galatia having been kept by the Holy Spirit from preaching the word in the province of Asia. When they came to the border of Mysia, they tried to enter Bithynia, but the Spirit of Jesus would not allow them to. So they passed by Mysia and went down to Troas. During the night Paul had a vision of a man of Macedonia standing and begging him, 'Come over to Macedonia and help us.'" The "Come over and help us" ends with a pronoun *us*. And it matters.

Here was Paul, sure of where he wanted to go, never stopping for directions, but being stopped at every turn. Until he received God's vision for ministry. And in the vision he met *a person*, the man from Macedonia. There is a clear lesson from this story. Do not go plant a church if all you have is a vision for a particular kind of church, or because you think a particular city is "cool." You can only plant a church once you have a vision for the people. Part of being missional is to recognize that we are to go into a culture, engage the people of that culture, and plant a biblically faithful church for those people, all the while acknowledging that culture matters in the way we do ministry. Remember this: the how of church ministry is determined by the who, when, and where of culture.

So, when we "come over," it's important to remember that we are going into our own community, not someone else's. It's so easy to hear an incredible speaker at a conference and say, "I'm going to be just like that pastor!" That is not the right goal, nor is it what God is calling you to be. Too often we get so excited by someone else's church that we get a vision for their church before we get a vision for our people.

The challenge made by this book is don't plant a church in your head. Plant a church in your community. When you are there, that's when the gospel transforms real people who are living real lives. When we are in love with someone else's community, we fall prey to community lust and demographic envy. We begin thinking, "If I could just be in this part of California, or this part of Seattle, or this part of Manhattan . . . then my church would be incredible." Know and live in your culture, not someone else's. Don't just bring a model; bring the gospel. Create a church. Don't create a plan.

In this book Ben Arment describes and also shows us how to understand the receptivity of the ground where you are planting.

Most important, we must bring Christ, not just a church. Particularly not a way of doing church. Sometimes I think we get too excited about the fact that we're leading a church. That's great, as long as we remember that we're planting the gospel that creates a church. It's best for us to leave trendiness to a culture obsessed with social media and Nielsen ratings. The momentum and deep roots called for by the Bible, and thus by Ben, is not to be the most trendy or the most relevant but to be the most focused on eternal issues. We're planting the gospel so we bring Christ and not just the church. Being missional has to be tied into the mission of Jesus, to seek and save the lost.

Unlike the game Red Rover, we win when we get to stay with our new "team" and begin leading it in a new direction. Planters must first take the time to listen to the Spirit and respond appropriately to His call to the particular people He assigns to us. Then we can best respond to the call to "come over" and win them for the kingdom of God.

As you read *Church in the Making*, you will receive the counsel of a leader who values innovation and who understands church planting. In the pages that follow, you will find your plans for leadership tested and sharpened. But more important, you will be challenged and encouraged to become the church leader and the church planter God calls you to be.

—Ed Stetzer

INTRODUCTION

They are four of the most devastating words in the English language to a church planter. It's a phrase you often hear when successful church planters are asked how they did it. They don't mean to be hurtful, but the implication is clear.

Are you ready for it?

God is just blessing.

These four words deliver a silent indictment against any church planter who is struggling. They imply that if your church is not growing or reaching the masses for Christ, then God must not be blessing you.

How did church planting become such a spiritual crapshoot? Why is it that some churches fail while others succeed? How is it that prayerful, hardworking men and women who are called by God and filled with faith could fall flat on their faces? Why would God allow them to flounder?

While researching this book, I had a hard time getting the leaders of failed church plants to call me back. I was touching on a sensitive part of their lives. Unmet expectations, it seems, leave a terrible mark.

They've been wounded spiritually. They've been let down by people. They've been disappointed by God. They've moved on to the next thing and don't want to talk about the past. Do not disturb.

But I think I know why they're reluctant to talk.

Church planters often don't know what went wrong.

Figuring out what it takes to plant a successful church is a mystery that still eludes the experts. I've heard several organizations tout their high survival rates. But new churches don't often fail in year one . . . or year two, for that matter. It's usually in year four or five when the plant is out of the incubator and no longer being coddled by its sponsors. Hardly anyone notices they've vanished.

Sometimes churches with the most likely chance to succeed end up being the biggest catastrophes. In 2001 a team of six full-time staff members moved to California to start In Christ Community Church in Beverly Hills High School. They were backed by a million-dollar budget and a flagship church on the east coast. They launched with four hundred people and dissolved within six months.

Sometimes what doesn't work in one area succeeds in another. In the spring of 2001, Jeff Murphy launched Big Sky Church near Cumming, Georgia. The church climbed to a reasonable number of people before taking a rapid nose-dive in attendance and momentum. Discouraged and bruised, Jeff shut down the church five years later. He moved back to Columbus, Georgia, where he had ministered for years as a popular youth pastor at a megachurch. In January 2009 he launched My Church and drew 625 people the first Sunday. They had to go to two services on their second week of existence.

This book attempts to uncover the mystery of church planting. In fact, I believe there is no mystery at all. God has a plan for multiplying churches that is evident in the corners of Scripture and lived out in the stories of church plants everywhere. But the insights are found in places where no one has thought to look. We've shrouded them with spiritual answers and mythologized faith stories.

It's startling to think that church planting doesn't have to be as difficult as we've made it out to be. Church planting, it turns out, is remarkably organic.

In part 1 of this book, I write about "Good Ground." Every community has an established degree of spiritual receptivity. When you plant a church on fertile soil, it springs to life out of the community's readiness. When you plant a church on infertile soil, it chokes and gasps to survive. In this case, you have to stop planting and start cultivating. On what kind of soil are you planting?

In part 2, I write about "Rolling Rocks." The church is a social entity as much as it is a spiritual one. People don't care about your new church unless social momentum is on your side. The Scriptures are replete with examples of how God used social forces to propel the gospel and start new churches. Has your church captured social momentum?

And in part 3, I write about "Deep Roots." The vision for a new church can never be imported but is birthed out of the community. The most effective church planters have a strong connection to their mission fields and a deep loyalty among their team. Are you planting the church your community needs?

Let's begin the journey to discover what makes or breaks a new church before it starts.

Part 1

GOOD GROUND

1

TOUGH SOIL

They're Not Interested

In our first month of planting a church in a Virginia suburb outside of Washington, DC, my wife, Ainsley, and I ran into some downstairs neighbors in our apartment complex parking lot. He had just retired as a high-ranking officer in the air force, and she was finishing up her career as a Capitol Hill staffer. They were enduring apartment living for a short time while their new home was being built in Kiawah Island, South Carolina.

"I noticed you don't leave for work every day," he said to me with a tone of concern. "Are you independently wealthy?"

I had converted our spare bedroom into a makeshift office where I made phone calls and crafted outreach plans during the day. The room served as a third-story perch where I could look out over the parking lot and pray for people as they came and went to work each day. That's really all

I could do for work at that point. But from his perspective, I appeared to be unemployed.

"No," I said laughingly and then gave him what would be my first real presentation on the need for a new church in northern Virginia that would meet people where they were and help them discover Jesus. I have to admit, I nailed the pitch.

After reflecting on it a moment, he looked at me with all the seriousness of a military officer and said, "I don't think anyone here is interested in that."

Ouch.

His curt response surprised me more than it hurt me. Ainsley and I were far too optimistic about church planting to take him seriously. Our community had one of the largest concentrated populations in the country. Without question there was a huge need for a church that would communicate the gospel, and we were there to fill it.

But seven years later I had to admit that he was right. Most people weren't interested. We saw people give their hearts to Christ, we gathered a great community of believers, and we made some genuine spiritual impact on people's lives. But our community never stopped trying to spit us out of its mouth.

When we offered to volunteer at neighborhood events, they suspected our motives. When we asked the park authority for space to host an outdoor children's event, they didn't return our phone calls. When we asked the community center about renting meeting space, construction projects or regulations always prevented us from using it.

I felt like the unsuspecting participant on a Syfy channel reality show. The rejection was becoming absurd.

One summer our church purchased a booth at the county's largest festival to hand out thousands of stress balls, breath mints, and chip clips—all emblazoned with our church's Web address and service times. Most people accepted the gifts without a second thought. But I remember one lady who glanced down at the pack of mints, saw our church name, and handed it back to me with disgust. I muttered a hopeful, "They're just breath mints."

When it was all said and done, not a single person came to our church from the outreach. And the rejection wasn't for lack of awareness.

Three days before Easter one year, the *Washington Post* published a full-page article about our church's unique worship environment in a movie theater. We couldn't have gotten better publicity if I had written it myself. The article ran on page 3, was hugely complimentary, and the photos made our church look full and exciting. It was our big break. It was the *Washington Post*, for crying out loud. But no one ever came from the article.

It wasn't just the unbelievers who snubbed us. My encounters with local churchgoers usually ended with awkward silence or a condescending series of questions. Why didn't I just go to their church? Had I ever met their pastor? Was I aware of how awesome their church was? And my favorite question: So how are you supporting yourself?

What was I doing here again?

The Need Is Not Enough

Those of us who plant churches do it for the need. We see scores of people far from God, the inability of other churches to reach absolutely everyone, and the radical need for people in our communities to experience God's saving grace.

But let's get one thing straight: the need for our churches is not enough. We can have compassion for people who are far from God. We can eat, sleep, and breathe church plant-ing. We can have a divine calling to start a church. And we can point to demographic studies that show how fast our cities are growing. But none of these factors is enough to produce a growing congregation. There is a hidden X factor to successful church planting that eludes most planters.

The Church Planting Experience

For several years I helped my denomination assess church planters on a monthly basis. We evaluated them before they hit the field, reviewed them one year into the plant, and then assessed them every year thereafter for as long as they were on financial support. It was like being a social worker for welfare recipients.

After doing this for several years, I began to see a pattern emerge among most of them. It was uncanny how similar their life cycles would be. Here is what the typical evangeli-cal church-planting experience looked like from my vantage point:

The church planter comes up with a great vision that in his mind measures up to Bill Hybels's seeker model or Rick Warren's baseball diamond. He's got flowcharts, demo-graphic studies, and even a facility picked out for when he starts holding services. The church exists perfectly in his mind before he ever steps foot in the community.

At the beginning of the process, the church planter is full of faith and determination. You can always tell a new, inex-perienced church planter because he's the only one who thinks he knows what he's doing. The veterans show a humil-ity that can only come from experience. It takes a year or two to knock the self-reliance out of the new guys.

Six months later the planter is still optimistic, but he's taken a few hits from early setbacks. Some potential core group members dropped out, he didn't get as much funding as he needed, or the worship leader he recruited got another job out of state.

By sheer optimism the planter pushes on. And it gives him great satisfaction finally to set a launch date that will deliver him into the land of milk and honey, a fast-growing church plant with a building campaign. If he could just start meeting weekly, the people would come. He's sure of it. The vision is too great.

He works up to the launch date by meeting with his core team. They're clueless about church planting, but he assures them they've got the right leader. So he makes them all read Erwin McManus's latest book and learn to run sound equipment. They hand out water bottles imprinted with their church logo at the grocery store and buy down people's gas at the corner Exxon. Everyone they meet acts interested in the new church, which gives them reason to be hopeful, but there's no telling who will actually show up on Sunday.

When the grand opening day finally arrives, the planter can't believe how many friends and family members attend. He'll have to disclose the number of "legitimate guests" to his ministry friends later on, but for now it creates the sort of excitement a first Sunday needs.

Amid the crowd there's a handful of first-time guests who seem to enjoy the service. As they leave, they promise to come back, and the church planter's got enough momentum to prepare for the second service.

What no one tells the planter is that attendance almost always drops by 50 percent on the second Sunday. The friends and family members go back to their home churches. Only a few guests come back. The core group begins to

realize that it's the same workload every Sunday, no matter
how many people attend. And many of the volunteers find
a good reason to skip out on the regular rotation—job sched-
ules, out-of-town guests, sickly mothers-in-law—take your
pick.

A year goes by, and before the church planter knows it,
the honeymoon is over. When people ask him how the
church is going, he pads his answers with words like *faithfulness, perseverance,* and the ever popular *God is teaching me so
much.*

It's only a matter of time before the planter is questioning his calling. Frustration starts creeping into his sermons.
And his wife, although supportive, admits to herself that she
wouldn't be all that upset if he decided to quit.

But the planter has heard too many legendary pastors
describe the difficulty of ministry and cringes at the idea of
being a quitter. What about Bill Hybels's emotional train
wreck in the early Willow years? He didn't give up. And
what about Rick Warren? Didn't he ask God to let him pastor one church for the rest of his life? That sounds so noble.

But the reality is the church planter sits in the front row
each week during worship because he can't bear to see how
few people there are behind him. He gets that sunken feeling at 10:10 a.m. every Sunday when he realizes no one else
is coming. And he begins to wonder if putting out all those
church signs along the road actually does any good. He
would never admit this, but it practically embarrasses him to
have guests visit the church.

By this time the church planter is a mess. He's defeated
and discouraged, possibly depressed. And he's formed all
sorts of new conclusions about God that hinder his faith.
What's worse is the planter, for the life of him, cannot pin-
point what went wrong. He blames himself; maybe he wasn't

cut out to be a pastor. He blames his circumstances; there simply wasn't a good meeting location. He blames bad decisions; he shouldn't have launched so soon. Or he blames other people; there was a divisive family out to turn everyone against him.

The truth is, most church planters never really know what went wrong. The worship wasn't stellar, but it wasn't bad either. The children's areas were makeshift, but the volunteers were welcoming. The preaching, the outreach, the location—who knows what went wrong?

When the planter eventually decides to quit, as most of them do, it's for a whole number of possibilities, but the real reason can never be defined. All he really knows is that he cannot go on and maintain his sanity or keep his family together. The emotional and spiritual toll have robbed him from a healthy ministry.

A Vicious Cycle

While white-water rafting down the New River in West Virginia years ago, our tour guide pointed out the skeletal remains of a deer caught under some rocks in a never-ending cycle of water. Apparently the deer got caught in the undertow and was unable to break free from the white-water trap. The guide said he watched for months as the never-ending undertow washed away the deer's composition.

That's a gruesome picture, I know. But I can't think of a better metaphor to describe the struggle of so many church planters. They're caught in a vicious cycle from which they can never seem to break free. From an outsider's perspective, their faithfulness appears noble. But on the inside these planters are slowly decomposing.

The Great Disillusionment

After listening to scores of church-planting stories like these in assessments and watching despondent pastors try to sort it all out while their wives fought back tears, I started asking God some serious questions: Why would he call people to undertake one of the most difficult challenges in ministry but let them struggle? Why would he listen to them beg and plead for people's souls, something so righteous and noble, but withhold his sovereign hand? Doesn't God want us to plant new churches? Doesn't he want us to grow his kingdom? If so, why doesn't he help?

For many people church planting is a disillusioning experience. The success of other planters appears to be utterly random, and the most unlikely people seem to enjoy the greatest fruit. For those of us who have been through it, church planting can feel like one big crapshoot, a game of Russian roulette with our own sanity. There's no telling whether we'll succeed or fail until we actually do it.

But here's what I discovered: successful church planting is not random. And it doesn't have to be mysterious. I believe Jesus gave us all the insight we need to plant successful churches and avoid disillusionment.

The answer lies under your feet.

2

SPIRITUAL FERTILITY

A Church Planting Mystery Unveiled

Church planting doesn't have to be such a mysterious let-down. We don't have to charge full-on after God's calling with idealistic enthusiasm and reckless abandon, only to fall flat on our faces. After the church gets off the ground, we don't have to settle for the agony of fruitlessness, spending year after year hoping our breakthrough is coming.

For years I felt like the captain of a sailboat without any wind. I carried out the spiritual equivalent of reshuffling deck chairs and rehearsing sailing maneuvers with my crew just to feel productive.

Church planters are good at this. When people aren't coming through our doors, we can stay incredibly busy writing membership class curriculum, redesigning the Web site for the fourth time, and drafting e-mail newsletters. But it's all futile. These things have little to do with our objective, and without people there is no true productivity about them.

But it doesn't have to be this way.

Jesus unveiled spiritual mysteries through the stories he told. The parables of the yeast, the mustard seed, the talents weren't just illustrations. They provided accurate metaphors for communicating hidden truths. Those without spiritual yearnings were simply entertained. But those who had ears to hear were enlightened.

Eyes to See

Several years ago a blind young man named Alex attended our church for a short time. In some strange way ministering to him helped justify our church's existence. There's just something about caring for the same needs mentioned in the Gospels. You don't see Jesus exorcising Lexus payments or healing corporate downsizing, which is what most of us pastors deal with today.

One Sunday my family spent a few minutes catching up with Alex after the service. At the time my son Wyatt was just a baby, six months old at the most, and I was holding him in my arms. As we talked with Alex, he knelt down to talk to Wyatt, who he thought was standing next to us. Alex didn't know how old he was. He'd never seen him.

He leaned down to my kneecap and said, "Hey buddy, how are you doing?"

This put me in an awkward position because I didn't want to embarrass him. So I dropped down with Wyatt until we met Alex's attention. Reaching out, I took hold of Alex's hand and pulled it toward Wyatt's little body. I carefully moved his fingers across Wyatt's face and ears so he could feel how small my son really was. I wanted to make my invisible son visible to Alex through his sense of touch.

This is what Jesus was trying to accomplish with parables. Spiritual truths are invisible to us. We can't see the kingdom of God so it's extremely hard to live by its principles. By telling us stories, Jesus was, in effect, taking us by the hand and helping us see invisible truths.

The key to successful church planting feels mysteriously hidden. But I'm convinced Jesus gave us all the insights we need. For those who have ears to hear, he took all of the mystery out of it.

The Idea of Success

Before I go any further, I want to talk about the idea of successful church planting. Of course, God is responsible for our success. And ultimately only he decides what is successful. But I want to point out that according to Scripture, successful churches grow numerically. Just look at how Luke records the growth of the early church in the book of Acts:

- "The number of people who were together was about 120" (1:15).
- "That day about 3,000 people were added to them" (2:41).
- "Every day the Lord added to them those who were being saved" (2:47).
- "The number of the men came to about 5,000" (4:4).
- "Believers were added to the Lord in increasing numbers" (5:14).
- "The number of the disciples was multiplying" (6:1).
- "The number of the disciples . . . multiplied" (6:7).
- "A large number . . . believed" (11:21).

- "Large numbers of people were added to the Lord" (11:24).
- "All who had been appointed . . . believed" (13:48).
- "Made many disciples" (14:21).
- "Churches . . . increased in number" (16:5).
- "Many of the Corinthians . . . believed" (18:8).
- "All the inhabitants of . . . Asia . . . heard the word" (19:10).
- "Many thousands" (21:20).

The only ones who dismiss numerical growth as an indicator of success are those who don't want it to matter for their own sakes. Otherwise they can't justify their static churches, and that would utterly devastate them.

I should know; I lived with this agony for years.

The most ardent critics of church growth are those whose churches aren't growing. Even those who don't believe in church growth principles experience growth when all of the right conditions are in place.

If your church is not growing, admit that something is not working. It's the only way to break free from the vicious cycle of fruitlessness.

The Parable of the Soil Types

I am convinced that the secret to successful church planting is found in the spiritual fertility of your community. In Matthew 13:3–9, Jesus tells a parable that explains what spiritual fertility looks like:

> "Consider the sower who went out to sow. As he was sowing, some seeds fell along the path, and the birds came and ate them up. Others fell on rocky ground, where there wasn't much soil, and they sprang up

quickly since the soil wasn't deep. But when the sun came up they were scorched, and since they had no root, they withered. Others fell among thorns, and the thorns came up and choked them. Still others fell on good ground, and produced a crop: some 100, some 60, and some 30 times what was sown. Anyone who has ears should listen!"

As Jesus explains later in this chapter, the seed represents the Word of God. You'll notice that the seed's fruitfulness depends on the fertility of the soil, which represents people's hearts. Of course the Word of God is powerful and sufficient enough to produce fruit on its own. But the barrier is the human heart. The gospel seed will only produce fruit in good ground.

Let me be clear about this: your ability to share the gospel effectively with someone depends on that person's heart condition. The seed of the gospel has all the power it needs to bear fruit. It's ready to transform lives. But if it falls on tough soil, it's as good as birdseed.

A Fertile Fellow

One time a young Hispanic man came to our church at the invitation of his roommate. He was a bright, entrepreneurial, single guy supporting his family back in Bolivia. After several visits to our church, he asked if he could meet me for coffee. Uh-oh.

I spent the next few days trying to figure out which argument against the Christian faith he would bring up. I skimmed *The Case for Christ*, the doctrines of the Catholic church, even the *Book of Mormon*, just in case.

By the time our coffee appointment arrived, I was like a boxer on fight day. I was amped up, prayed up, and ready for anything he could swing at me. The only problem was I hadn't prepared in the slightest for what he was about to ask me.

Between swigs of a caramel macchiato, he looked at me and asked, "So how do I become a Christian?"

That was his first and only question. I was floored. Here I had been preparing to defend the Christian faith from the attacks of relativism and Mormonism, and this guy asks me how to become a Christian. I would dare say that my Bolivian friend's heart was spiritually fertile. It was a tender seedbed, waiting for the gospel to take root. He didn't know what he was asking for, but he knew he wanted it. He was yearning for it. Talk about a fertile fellow.

Ear to the Ground

Jesus had his — *"You* — *to have your ear to the ground!"*

Jesus' ministry was to the spiritually fertile. When he called Matthew to follow him, it's because he had seen a glimmer of tenderness in this man's gruff exterior while passing by his tax collection booth. When he met Nicodemus in that darkened alley, he must have seen the religious shell around his heart beginning to crack. Jesus took the forbidden path through Samaria with his disciples because he knew about a prepared prostitute who drew water there.

Of course, Jesus had his fair share of tough soil too. The rich young ruler had a few too many thorns corrupting his heart. Remember the angry townsfolk who preferred demons over losing their pig population? Tough soil. And when Jesus climbed mountains to teach his followers, he wasn't trying to conduct team-building exercises. He was avoiding the spiritually disinterested.

Fertile Communities

Not only is your ability to share the gospel dependent upon a person's heart condition, but your ability to plant a church successfully is dependent upon your community's spiritual fertility as well. Just as different communities take on various language dialects, cultural customs, and values, so they have varying degrees of spiritual receptivity. It would sound absurd if it weren't so biblical.

In Matthew 11:21, Jesus shares his view of spiritual infertility within communities:

> "Woe to you, Chorazin! Woe to you, Bethsaida! For if the miracles that were done in you had been done in Tyre and Sidon, they would have repented in sackcloth and ashes long ago!"

Here Jesus is comparing the spiritual receptivity of four towns. Two of them were clearly more fertile than the others. This happens several other times in Scripture. Jesus knew how to spot fertile territory.

It never dawns on most church planters that their target community already has an established degree of spiritual fertility.

A Tale of Two Town Centers

My family and I just spent a year living in Georgia. We moved from Reston, Virginia, which is known to city planners throughout the world for its world-class town center. The first time we saw its Parisian fountain, outdoor ice-skating rink, high-end retail shops, and high-rise luxury condos, the community captivated us.

But throughout our time there, our church plant was practically shunned from reaching out to the community.

Handing out water bottles, posting flyers, hosting festivals—
all of the usual church planting fare was strictly prohibited.
To care for people at the hospital, I was required to meet the
approval of an ecumenical priest who forbade any talk of
Jesus. We offered volunteers, sound equipment, and even
money to support the community's festivals and events, but
they weren't interested.

Compare that to an experience we had during our first
month in Georgia. Our family was visiting a local town center during a community festival. It was packed full of townspeople, games for children, and sponsored booths, not unlike
the ones in Reston. But there was one significant difference.
A local Baptist church had major billing at the event. Their
signs were posted everywhere; their volunteers ran most of
the activities; and the public-address announcer thanked
them repeatedly for their service. We were clearly in a different pot of soil.

Some communities are simply more spiritually fertile
than others. These communities are practically begging for a
new church. The people's hearts have been prepared, and
the community leaders are accommodating. When the
planter needs meeting space, businessmen offer their facilities for free. When he needs remodeling done, Christian sub-
contractors suddenly become available. When the planter
interacts with waitresses and bank tellers, they're willing to
give the church a try.

It's as if they're just waiting for a church planter to come
along and start something.

The Plant before the Planter

Several years ago I got a phone call from a banker near
Richmond, Virginia, who wanted to know where he could

find a church planter. No one had ever asked me that question before, so I asked for clarification.

"I'm part of a church that's looking for a planter," he explained. "A group of about fifty of us have come together to start a church, but we don't have a pastor yet."

I couldn't believe my ears. My only experience with church planting had been moving to a God-forsaken location where it didn't appear that anyone wanted another church. To think fifty people were waiting, praying, and searching for a church planter blew my mind.

But this is how it works in fertile places. People are practically asking for the church plant. They may not be saying the actual words like this fellow, but they've been spiritually prepared to look for one.

Fertile Scenarios

No one ever told me that church planting could be this easy. And that's probably because no one ever told my mentors in church planting about the principle of spiritual fertility. I'll give you a few examples. Each of these scenarios comes from a real experience I've witnessed over the past ten years. All of them produced thriving, growing ministries in a natural and organic way.

Familiarity

A church planter went back to his hometown where he'd built relationships for most of his life. He was the high school football star. He knew the guys at the barbershop from years of Saturday-morning haircuts. He knew the local churches better than anyone and where the pockets of spiritual fertility were located. He faced nothing but open doors everywhere he went. His brother was a city councilman after all.

Heritage

A town had a strong spiritual heritage that was lying dormant. You could tell just by driving down Main Street. The downtown area was lined with old, traditional church buildings that were now just a shell of their former glory. There was even a Christian college nearby. Everyone's grandmother went to church, but the next generation had stopped going. When this church planter started a fresh, new work, the community came alive again. The spiritual heritage that was lying dormant reawakened to produce a massive revival.

Seasoning

One community had been visited by a young, itinerant evangelist for years. He was a beloved youth speaker and popular camp evangelist. He saw tremendous spiritual fruit result from his ministry. After numerous visits he developed a love for the community and a burden for its people. By the time he started a church, there were scores of supporters waiting to follow his lead.

Blessing

A veteran youth pastor decided to plant a church in the same town as his home church. He had hinted to his pastor about it for years and now had his blessing. Many of the teenagers who grew up loving him were now young adults and eager to join his new endeavor. The mother church sent people, resources, and financial support to give the plant a new boost. Within a year the new church was not only self-supporting; it was thriving.

Prayer

Several old ladies had been praying for the high school in their hometown for years. They asked God over and over to bring someone to start a Young Life program for students. When God finally brought a newly married couple to start the ministry, the high school was spiritually ready. The administration and teachers' hearts had been prepared by the power of these women's prayers. The program took off.

Remnant

A church planter "worked the soil" for a few years but ultimately decided to call it quits. He left behind a small community of believers who wanted to continue the work. They were primed and ready for a leader with fresh vision. God brought a young planter who fit the need. He built on a foundation that had already been established and took the church to a whole new level.

A Difficult Row to Hoe

On the other hand, some communities are not spiritually fertile at all. When church planters tackle these locations, they run into resistance, apathy, and even hostility.

Planting a church in a spiritually infertile community can be done, but it's like walking up an escalator that's going down. It's difficult. And I don't mean difficult in a "ministry is hard" kind of way. For example, every pastor has to deal with critical people. But a pastor who has to deal with critical people when he can't reach many of them to begin with is a different kind of hard.

I'm not saying we should only plant churches in spiritually fertile places. Far from it. We need the gospel to penetrate hard-to-reach places. And many of us are called to go there. After all, the point of planting a church is to evange-lize a community. But to spend year after year struggling to reach people, only to burn out and finally quit the church is tragic. It doesn't have to be this way.

If you're in this situation, failing is not your only option.

3

CULTIVATION

Failure Is Not the Only Option

Failure is not the only option for a struggling church plant. We don't have to crash and burn, give up the dream, and apply for a job at the car dealership. Nor do we have to live in the agony of trying to build an organization that's just not coming together. There is another option that almost all struggling church planters fail to see.

It's called cultivation.

When a new church struggles year after year to see fruit from its activity, we should assume it's not quite time to plant. Instead, there is tilling, watering, and cultivating to be done.

Let's continue the agricultural metaphor. If you keep planting seeds that produce no fruit, you've either got bad seeds or bad soil. And because we know from Romans 1:16 that the gospel seeds are never lacking in power to save, it must always be the soil. Every time. But do we have to surrender to the soil and just deal with what we've got? Absolutely not.

Here's the thing: I believe the parable of soil types is not just *descriptive*. In other words, Jesus wasn't just telling us that sometimes it works out and sometimes it doesn't. Rather, the parable was *instructive*. That is, Jesus was telling us what to do when we find ourselves on tough ground. Why else would he go to such lengths to describe each soil type? Look at his explanation in Matthew 13:19–23:

> "When anyone hears the word about the kingdom and doesn't understand it, the evil one comes and snatches away what was sown in his heart. This is the one sown along the path. And the one sown on rocky ground— this is one who hears the word and immediately receives it with joy. Yet he has no root in himself, but is short-lived. When pressure or persecution comes because of the word, immediately he stumbles. Now the one sown among the thorns—this is one who hears the word, but the worries of this age and the seduction of wealth choke the word, and it becomes unfruitful. But the one sown on the good ground—this is one who hears and understands the word, who does bear fruit and yields: some 100, some 60, some 30 times what was sown."

I've heard people interpret this parable as "Just be faithful in sharing the gospel. God will take care of the results." But let me ask you this: If we were just meant to be faithful in sharing the gospel, why would we have to know the reasons for bad soil? Why would Jesus give us this insight if we weren't supposed to do something about it?

Tending Hearts

We don't actually change people's hearts. That's God's job. But we can help remove the man-made inhibitors to the gospel.

The hardness of people's hearts is often caused by circumstances in life—a broken home, sexual abuse, the death of a loved one, divorce. They're tragic events, but they do not have to turn someone away from Christ forever. Tough soil can be cultivated once again.

You would never say that your own spiritual growth is entirely dependent on God. If I asked God to help me escape the sin of lust but kept watching porn, he couldn't do much to help me. However, if I installed Web site blockers, cut off certain cable channels, and got an accountability partner, now we're talking. God has room to work. That's cultivation.

Think about people who grew up with abusive fathers and cannot see God as anything but uncaring. They can't open their hearts to him, let alone call him "Father." Now is it only God's job to restore their trust in him, or might we be able to help cultivate their hearts through a caring friendship?

What about the woman who had a terrible experience in church and now won't step foot anywhere near one? Is it only God's responsibility to restore her? Or is there something you and I can do?

Cultivation Comes before Sowing

The day I wrote this chapter, I had coffee in Irvine, California, with Cue Jean-Marie, the pastor of causes at Newsong Church. Cue is a former rapper for Virgin Records who came from a life of drugs and thugs with Tupac Shakur to now leading a church in the central Los Angeles skid row district.

He told me the story of visiting a church where a young lady was given the opportunity to share her testimony. Surprisingly she used the opportunity to announce her role in the sex industry. She unashamedly called herself a "ho" and explained that she wanted to advocate the rights of sex trade workers and prevent the criminalization of their profession.

Cue said he cringed as the pastor squeezed her arm and announced in front of the entire congregation that he wanted to tell her "what they were about." The pastor and another member of the congregation spent the next hour preaching against prostitution. At the end of their tirade, the prostitute said she didn't need to "be saved" and apologized for having come to their church in the first place. She left without ever being seen again.

Cue told me he wondered what might have happened if the pastor had asked what led to her life on the streets. Cue wondered if she might have opened her heart if they had opened their ears. Who knows, she might have come back and brought her friends with her. Now we'll never know.

But one thing was certain: at that moment she wasn't prepared to hear the gospel. And now she might not ever be.

As trite as it sounds, she didn't care what they believed because she didn't believe they cared. The gospel is much better received when people's hearts have been cultivated.

Necessary Offenses Versus Unnecessary Offenses

I know what you're thinking. The gospel is a stumbling block, an offense to sinful people. It's an indictment on our fallen condition. And you're right. But many unnecessary offenses have been attached to the gospel that must be removed.

These include the patronizing tone in which some people explain their beliefs, the condemnation we emphasize over God's grace, and the religious activity we substitute for faith. These are all weeds that must be removed from the soil of people's hearts to cultivate a place for the gospel.

The Little, Yellow Plane

I'll bet you've heard the story of Jim Elliott. In 1956 he and four other men—Ed McCully, Roger Youderian, Pete Fleming, and their pilot, Nate Saint—attempted to make contact with the violent Huaorani Indians deep in the jungles of Ecuador. They circled the village for months in a little, yellow airplane trying to get a glimpse of the hidden natives. Each time they flew, they dangled a gift at the end of a long string as a peace offering. They even figured out how to make the gift hang above the ground within arm's reach by flying in concentric circles around the drop site.

Eventually the tribesmen not only took the gift, but they returned gifts of their own to the missionaries as well—a good sign.

The rest of the story is tragic but glorious. After watching the plane land on a sandy bank at the edge of the jungle, the Huaorani killed all five men and let their corpses float down the Curaray River.

However, their death opened a door for the missionaries' wives to enter the village unharmed. Elizabeth Elliott and the other women used the death of their husbands to demonstrate the grace and forgiveness that can only be found in Jesus Christ.

The Huaorani people were forever changed by this experience, and many of them are following Jesus to this day. In fact, the man who killed Nate Saint travels around the world with his victim's son, Nate Jr., to tell his story of forgiveness and redemption. And it all started with a yellow airplane.

Now if cultivation is not our job, then what was that?

Curing Atheism

When we cultivate people's hearts, we are not trying to sell people on following Christ. We are simply removing the man-made thorns that keep them from trusting him. I wouldn't believe it could work if I hadn't seen it for myself.

In our first year of marriage, my wife, Ainsley, and I spent most of our evenings at Starbucks drinking hot chocolate and reading good books.

One of the baristas gave us a hard time about our choice of books, which were mainly spiritual ones. Her name was Erin, and she was an atheist. Erin had fiery red hair, a brash mouth, and a wild lifestyle. She spoke candidly about her sexual adventures and her defiance against anything religious. She also cussed like a sailor. But on her breaks Erin would come over to our table to talk. Within a few months we were solid friends.

This was our first year of marriage, so Ainsley and I had grandiose plans of entertaining friends in our tiny apartment. We'd light candles, serve dinner, and create a cozy space for our friends to hang out. We invited Erin to join us on numerous occasions. She felt comfortable in our place, laughed with us, and trusted us to be honest but not judgmental.

One evening we had a better than usual conversation with Erin about matters of faith. When we met Erin, her heart was like a brick wall. She refused to believe in God, let alone put her trust in Jesus. But on this night we noticed that her heart was beginning to soften. She revealed her disappointing encounters with the church, her father's diagnosis with cancer, and some of her other personal struggles. Ainsley and I knew it was time to plant a seed.

I admit I got this tactic from a book, but I said, "Erin, why don't you pray and ask God to prove his existence to you? You don't have to say anything else. And if there is no God, you haven't lost anything. Just try it and see what happens."

She didn't promise to do it, but Ainsley and I continued to pray for her.

Several months later Erin was back at our house for a party. She stayed after everyone left and asked if she could speak with us. We sat on the couch as she fidgeted awkwardly and said, "Remember how you told me to ask God to prove himself to me? Well, I did. And I don't want to tell you how he did it, but he did."

Tears began falling down her cheeks as we invited her to trust Jesus. She prayed with us in that moment, and her life was forever changed.

Throughout my time as a pastor and a church planter, I have experienced stories of cultivation like this over and over again. We discovered that friendship goes a long way to prepare someone's heart for the gospel.

When people's hearts are hardened, our job is not over. We don't have to walk away in resignation. We can help nurture the soil of their hearts until there's a soft, receptive place for the gospel seed to plant deep roots.

Cultivation Is Biblical

This is exactly what the apostle Paul did. As we can see in the book of Acts, Paul cultivated a mission field before he dared to plant churches. He traveled from city to city, preaching in synagogues, interacting with townspeople, debating with scholars, and slowly but surely winning followers of Jesus.

But then he left town.

When he returned on a second journey, Paul would gather the growing believers, appoint elders, and make them an official congregation. After this his follow-up visits were intended to strengthen and encourage them. But notice that the church was only planted after the seeds of the gospel had taken root and a core group had formed.

Paul was so much of a cultivator that he refused to plant churches in places where others had cultivated. He said in Romans 15:20, "My aim is to evangelize where Christ has not been named, in order that I will not be building on someone else's foundation."

What is this foundation? It's the work of cultivation. Just look at how Paul describes his ministry in 1 Corinthians 3:6: "I planted, Apollos watered, but God gave the growth." Paul rightfully credits God for producing the fruit, but he makes no apologies for doing the work of planting the seed.

Growing Soybeans in Wheat Season

Most church planters hit the field without any awareness of spiritual fertility. So they can't figure out what's wrong when nothing comes from their efforts.

A farmer would be crazy to drive a combine through a field twelve months out of the year. He has to prepare the soil and plant seeds before he can harvest a crop. Likewise, a church planter must understand the right time to launch a congregation. Just like farming, there are two activities for church planters: cultivating and planting. If you do the right thing in the wrong season, you get zero results.

We have to be careful about church growth conferences. Just because a particular pastor is experiencing a bountiful harvest doesn't mean it's the right time for us. Different communities have different levels of fertility. Yet we go to conferences as if we're trying to learn how to harvest soybeans in wheat season. It just doesn't work. And we end up with farmers who think they're failures.

I'm convinced that Jesus' statement in John 4:35—"the fields . . . are ready for harvest"—is the most dangerously misinterpreted passage for church planters in the Bible. We assume this means that people everywhere are ready to accept Christ at any given time. We just need to be faithful. But Jesus was describing the nearness of the end of the age. He wasn't saying that communities are always receptive to salvation.

Jesus was always aware of spiritual fertility. He walked away from his hometown of Nazareth because his friends and family members weren't prepared to see him as divine. The whole reason he introduced the Jewish nation to the law was to prepare them for saving grace. And after they rejected him, it was only then that he planned to go to the Gentiles, as we see in Acts 13:46. The Scriptures say there will be a time yet again when many Jews will be prepared to respond.

It was all about spiritual preparedness for Jesus.

The How of Cultivation

Throughout my experience of planting a church in tough soil, I watched God use our congregation to cultivate the community from resistant to mildly receptive. By the end of

my seven-year stretch, community leaders were starting
to warm up to us, facilities were becoming available, and
we were getting invited to host a booth in the community
festival.

Here are six ways to cultivate people's hearts:

1. Pray for them like crazy. The Holy Spirit will go
    before you to prepare the hearts of people. He
    responds to prayer by softening their hearts.
    Cultivating through prayer is like walking on a
    people mover at the airport: you're the one walking,
    but each step takes you further than you could go
    on your own.

2. Create a financial model that is not dependent on
    the people you're reaching. We want to help people
    experience the blessing of financial stewardship. But
    if our churches immediately face money struggles,
    we'll sabotage the work of cultivation. Unprepared
    people will think we just want their money. It's
    better to draw outside support or even work a
    second job to take the pressure off our mission field.

3. Understand that every encounter with someone
    matters. Cultivation includes run-ins at the grocery
    store, random acts of kindness, and even dinner with
    friends. We don't have to speak the gospel in every
    encounter. In fact, unless they're asking about it,
    they're probably not ready to hear it. Don't cast
    that seed just yet.

4. Be committed for the long haul. Cultivating a
    community is not a short-term project. Many
    successful church planters in difficult areas have
    been there for twenty years or longer.

5. Build strong friendships with a high degree of trust.
    People want to know you're a friend, not a

missionary. Once you establish some trust, you'll be able to say much more than you could as a stranger.

6.   Know that you'll have to restore Christianity's reputation first. People with hardened hearts are starting out with a negative impression of Christians. Your job is to get them from, say, a negative seven or a negative three to at least a neutral zero on the continuum of receptivity. If you can put Christians back in the plus one category by your own lifestyle, you've done a great work to start.

Less Organization, More Organism

In your spiritual geography you must either be a cultivator or a planter. What you do will be determined by your area's soil type. It's either time to plant a church or time to cultivate people's hearts. If you dive headlong into planting a church on tough soil, you'll get discouraged quickly and burn out.

Can you cultivate soil while you're planting a church? Absolutely. Church planters must constantly build relationships with people. But I'm talking about the primary focus of our efforts. When the church plant is not working, we must stop trying to build an organization and start connecting with people in a more organic way.

Shamed into Clarity

One Saturday I was studying for a sermon outside a coffee shop. To be honest, I was discouraged about having to preach to so few people that next morning. I was questioning my calling, the church's purpose. I was a mess. But out of the blue two teenagers sheepishly approached me. They nervously forced out a question.

"Sir, would you mind if we asked you a few questions for a survey we're doing?"

I looked down at the Bibles in their hands and knew immediately what they were doing. For the next five minutes they asked me about my faith and what I believed about Jesus. They were part of a youth group preparing for a mission trip and were practicing evangelism in their own local community.

I wanted to crawl in a hole and die. Here I was, a church planter, griping and complaining about how few people were coming to my church, while these two kids were doing something about it. The sense of shame I experienced that day sparked a big change in me. No longer did I put all of my efforts into building an organization that obviously wasn't coming together. Instead, I shifted toward the work of cultivation.

Where to Start Cultivating

It's important to know what your community needs more, cultivating or planting, because each requires something different from you. And you will have to evaluate your effectiveness in completely different ways.

You may feel a strong pressure to go as quickly as you can from cultivation to planting because planting feels more productive. Cultivation doesn't have an immediate payoff. We can't show off our amazing speaking ability or impress people with a worship band. But the secret to successful church planting lies in the work of cultivation. Without a prepared community, all of our efforts can be futile.

Another reason we quickly jump into planting is because cultivation seems humanly impossible. As we face the thorns and tough soil around us, we can feel that making a difference is impossible. Where do we start? We'd much rather have people come to us than have to go to them.

But Jesus gave us insight on where to begin. Let's go there now.

4

PEOPLE OF PEACE

Strangers on Foreign Soil

When Ainsley and I started a church just over a year into our marriage, we had no idea what was in store for us. We've always been idealistic about the future. Even in premarital counseling, we got strong marks for compatibility but drew red flags for being too naïve about the difficulty of marriage. We went into church planting with the same optimistic spirit, and it almost killed us.

Moving to Reston was like living in another country. Our cost of living tripled, the pace of life was faster, and the people were too occupied with their jobs on Capitol Hill to think about church. Spiritually they were a whole different species. Relativism was the prevailing spiritual belief. Nobody was wrong; everyone was right. That's a tough audience for someone with the exclusive claims of the gospel.

A few megachurches served as the default go-to churches for any Christians who moved to the area. But their pastors had grown cynical about the parade of young pastors who came through town. There had been so many fly-by-night church planters that we amounted to nothing more than snake oil salesmen who stayed only as long as business was good.

During my time in Reston, I watched more than ten church plants come and go. They were like bottle rockets that shot off quickly but came crashing down when the fireworks were over. It's no wonder the community wouldn't take us seriously. I was set up for rejection from the minute I got there.

I did everything I could to get a foothold in our community. I smiled at strangers at gas stations, hoping for a conversation. Ainsley and I signed up for trial gym memberships, attended birthday parties for people we'd never met, and flitted from hair salon to hair salon hoping for a connection.

My one attempt at reaching the business community was a complete disaster. I had signed up to host a John Maxwell simulcast featuring Lou Holtz and a series of other leadership experts live via satellite. I pounded the pavement for months trying to find businesspeople to attend. I called Amway salespeople, real estate agents, and even former senators. On the day of the event, there were only eight of us in that rented hotel ballroom—my wife, my cable guy, and the five friends he invited with the free tickets I gave him.

Ordained Friends — *Carole, Real Person*

Amid these impossible beginnings, God confirmed our calling to Reston through several ordained relationships. On our first trip to find an apartment, a real estate agent named Carol offered her services. Carol was one of the highest earning real estate agents in Reston. She was a socialite in the community, a philanthropist, and a bleeding-heart relativist.

She saw value in every religion and refused to believe that Jesus was the only way to God. In other words, she was the most unlikely person for God to use in our lives.

But to our shock and amazement, God moved her heart to care for us deeply. She saw two punk kids trying to make it in the big city, and we instantly became endeared to her. In spite of the actual paying customers she could have been helping, she spent two solid days driving us around to cheap rental properties with no hope of commission. Occasionally we'd pull off into a parking lot and talk for a few hours about our lives. We made a powerful connection. And when we finally found an apartment we could afford, Carol paid the deposit to secure it for us.

For the next seven years, Carol made no adjustments in her spiritual convictions. She only came to our services on Christmas and Easter, still resisting the gospel we communicated. But I would dare say that God used her more than anyone else to provide for us during our time there. Even as we were moving away seven years later, Carol invited us to stay in her beautiful home on moving night and to lean on her for any needs. She wasn't a believer in the exclusive claims of Jesus, but she cared for us more deeply than any church we've attended.

Look for a Person of Peace

Before I talk about the other ordained relationships, I want to describe, in biblical terms, what was going on here. In Matthew 10:11–13, Jesus sends out his disciples in pairs to preach the kingdom of heaven and to heal people throughout various villages. He tells them to take nothing with them—no money, no extra clothes, and no shoes or sandals. But the next bit of instruction is an amazing insight for a church planter:

"When you enter any town or village, find out who is worthy, and stay there until you leave. Greet a household when you enter it, and if the household is worthy, let your peace be on it."

In essence, Jesus was instructing them to look for a Carol. We'll call this individual the "person of peace." This is someone God uses to help make your ministry possible. It's a relational foothold. They don't have to be Christians. Some are, some aren't. What distinguishes them, however, is their hospitality toward your ministry. They could be financial donors, businesspeople who offer up free services, well-connected individuals who introduce you to friends—you name it. But they are all God's agents, sometimes unknowingly, for making your ministry possible.

You need a person of peace. And when you find one, you'll know you're supposed to be there. If you're sent to a spiritually infertile area, you may only find one or two. If you're in a fertile area, you may find a whole core group waiting for you. Maybe your persons of peace are already surrounding you, and God is waiting for you to start a church.

They'll Be Asking for You

I'm going to say something highly controversial here, but please hear me out. We've made church planting much, much harder than it needs to be. When we submit to the natural process God created to get churches off the ground, it's actually pretty easy. Now I'm not saying that ministry is easy. We will be under constant spiritual attack when we're trying to further the kingdom of God. But growing churches is God's job. That's not our burden to bear.

God doesn't expect us to work the plant out of the ground. We are only to cultivate and plant seeds; God will take care of the rest. When the ground is hard, it's time to cultivate. When the ground is good, it's time to plant. And you can do both at the same time. But it's important to differentiate these activities to keep ourselves from burning out over failed expectations.

When the ground is good, Christian leaders will come around us to serve. People will be open to the gospel message. The community won't spit us out of its mouth, and they'll appreciate our acts of service and kindness. Doors will open. People won't literally say it, but they'll practically be asking for our churches.

A Few Exceptions

I want to make a few exceptions to this. Sometimes God will use hardship to shape a church planter's life, and so he prevents the growth. I personally went through a refining fire because of our slow start. By the end I was a more mature, Christ-dependent pastor.

Sometimes we haven't learned how to relate to our communities. It took me five years to think like a Restonian. My earliest attempts at ministry in this community were more suited for the Bible Belt. I had to detox from my past church experiences.

And sometimes God will use our struggle to inspire and impact others. Through blogging, writing articles, and speaking about my experience, I have been able to encourage hundreds if not thousands of struggling church planters. God might hinder a new church's growth for numerous reasons. But when all else is healthy, good seeds plus good ground equals a successful church plant.

Paul's Enablers

The apostle Paul understood the principle of the person of peace. Just look at where he went in each town he visited. His first stop was the synagogue where people were familiar with the Old Testament Scriptures. He tried to find connections through the established law. In pagan cities he went to the temples and lecture halls where he tried to connect through the poetry of the age. And in places without either one, he got creative.

Look with me at Acts 16:13–15. Here Luke describes how he and Paul found a person of peace in Philippi:

> On the Sabbath day we went outside the city gate by
> the river, where we thought there was a place of
> prayer. We sat down and spoke to the women gathered
> there. A woman named Lydia, a dealer in purple cloth
> from the city of Thyatira, who worshiped God, was
> listening. The Lord opened her heart to pay attention
> to what was spoken by Paul. After she and her
> household were baptized, she urged us, "If you
> consider me a believer in the Lord, come and stay at
> my house." And she persuaded us.

Lydia turned out to be an incredible person of peace for Paul. He found her where God-fearing people were known to pray. Lydia wasn't a believer when Paul found her, but she quickly accepted the message because she had a prepared heart. The same goes for Priscilla and Aquila. These people were God's chosen agents for making Paul's ministry possible. Without them Paul couldn't have found the relational footholds that are necessary for starting churches. He partnered with these friends to cultivate tough soil.

The List Goes On

Carol wasn't the only ordained relationship that God brought into our lives. There was Katherine, a believer who seemed to know anyone and everyone in northern Virginia. She invited us to parties so we could meet other people without looking stupid. In the early years of our church, almost every person who attended came through Kath's network of friends. She encouraged us through difficult times and stood by us through necessary changes that scattered other people.

A talented young man named Anthony came at Katherine's invitation and served with us in complete selflessness. He invited his network of friends to every church gathering, ran our audio and video equipment every week, and paid for much-needed resources out of his own pocket. When we launched our first service with seventy-two people, sixty of them were Anthony's friends.

Urban Legends

Often what keeps church planters from understanding the power of persons of peace are the stories of legendary churches. We think most of them sprang out of great leadership, a great vision from God, the authority of biblical preaching, and cultural relevance. And of course they did. But I don't know a single church planter who thinks he's missing these things.

Church planters are notorious for thinking that a great dream plus hard work equals a thriving church. But church planters fail all the time with this formula and have no idea why.

If you've ever read *The Purpose Driven Church*, you know the story of how Rick Warren prayed for a church to pastor for the rest of his life. He scoured maps in his basement for fast-growing areas and discovered Orange County. The icing on this mythical cake is that he sent a letter to a director of missions in California at the same time the director was sending a letter to him.

Now that's the stuff of which legends are made. What you probably don't know is that before Rick planted Saddleback Community Church, he attended and then taught at California Baptist University in Riverside, California. But not only this—he preached more than one hundred revivals throughout the Riverside area, which is just a thirty-minute drive from where the Saddleback campus currently sits. Do you think he might have helped cultivate this part of the country for a church plant? At the very least he had to be aware of the spiritual readiness of this area.

I don't mean to diminish this story because it truly is phenomenal. But I'm righteously indignant about the thousands of defeated church planters who have no idea what hit them. I'm sick of the mortality rate. I want to keep planters from thinking that all they need is a great vision and a fast-growing community to be successful. I want to assert that behind every great church is a cultivated community.

Please understand that spiritual fertility can vary within subcommunities and even within a few miles. One of the leaders at New Life Christian Church in Centreville, Virginia, told me they could successfully plant new churches anywhere to the south of their main campus. But a church plant just five miles to the north had trouble making it. They said the difference was the spiritual receptivity of the community. All of the other factors were the same.

Keep in mind that cultivated communities are more about relational networks than actual geography. For example, a city can have distinct subcultures that are more receptive than others. A spiritual topography lies hidden to the naked eye.

A New Way of Thinking

You could easily interpret what I'm saying to mean that we should only plant churches in fertile communities, but nothing could be further from the truth. If you are called to be a cultivator, then by all means go. I was one of them. We need missionaries in the toughest parts of the world. For most of us, this is exactly the mission field where God leads us. And the Bible teaches that the greatest rewards will be given to those who face persecution and difficulty for the cause of Christ.

But cultivating soil requires a different way of viewing ministry success. It's a long-term approach, and the mile markers of progress aren't exactly tangible. It's a breakthrough conversation or a sense of spiritual impact. It's a softening of the heart that may or may not translate into church attendance.

Billy Graham once said that it takes twenty people to lead someone to Christ. The first person thinks she had nothing to do with it. The last person thinks it was all him. The work of cultivation was those first nineteen people. And if they're not careful, they can think all their effort was all for nothing.

What I'm saying is to be aware of the soil conditions in which you are planting. Knowing this could save you from the discouragement and depression that so many planters experience. You'll know which activity to engage in— cultivating or planting—and you'll have far more patience with the spiritual process. It will save you from jealousy or anger. It will help you see your unique, God-given role in your target community. And if it turns out that a church doesn't come from your labor in the field, you won't beat yourself up about it or get angry with God.

After all, church planting is the only endeavor in the world with a built-in exit strategy.

5

EXIT STRATEGY

So-Called Faithfulness

Unfortunately we have placed a dangerous label on church planting that puts tremendous pressure on planters to persevere through any and all difficulties. We call it faithfulness. But in many cases it should really be called stupidity.

Maybe it's all those stories of noble martyrs from the first century that make us think we should endure any struggle less punishing than being burned alive at the stake. Or maybe it's the allure of having lifelong ministries in one place for which great men and women of God have prayed. But this pressure to toil and struggle for years on end under the banner of faithfulness is not only biblically unfounded; it's destroying church planters and their families as well.

Church planters rarely fail in the first year. They hardly ever fail in the second year. Church planters mostly fail in years three to five when their churches have drifted into obscurity, when the idealistic luster has worn off, and no one is paying attention to them anymore.

Just as grandparents eventually stop including five-dollar bills in their grandchildren's birthday cards, so the supporters stop sending start-up funds. At some point the church planter can no longer appeal to an exciting vision that clearly isn't happening, and the plague of discouragement begins.

I want to be clear about my righteous indignation at the destructive effects of this so-called faithfulness. Don't get me wrong: I believe wholeheartedly in being faithful to God. And I believe that faithfulness almost always requires great sacrifice and hardship. But I'm talking about something entirely different. I'm talking about activities that bring unnecessary difficulty into a pastor's life. It's self-imposed martyrdom.

Permission to Walk Away

A good friend from seminary happened to move to the same part of northern Virginia one year before I did. Eric was an incredible communicator; I know because I shared a homiletics class with him. And it was all we classmates could do to keep up with him. In fact, Eric was so good at preaching that the professor often invited him to speak at the church where he was serving as interim pastor. Only five of us could preach practice sermons per class, and I think all of us prayed to God that we didn't have to go on the same day as Eric.

After we graduated, we all went our separate ways. And unbeknownst to me, Eric ended up planting a church just eight miles from where Ainsley and I would eventually be planting. By the time we hit the field, I was relieved to discover we would be close. Northern Virginia was far enough from our family that we needed all the friends we could get.

Eric was the only one who helped us move into our new apartment, but somehow we fell out of contact for the next few years. As you probably know, it's easier for pastors across the country to get together than pastors down the street.

What I didn't realize was that Eric was struggling. His church launched with an impressive trajectory, but then things started falling apart. His good friend and worship leader abandoned him just one year into the plant. A close family member died at a young age. He had a daughter born with a disabling condition. And some leaders in his church started turning against him. Attendance at his church began plummeting, and he couldn't muster the energy to go after more. What was once a church of 140 had been whittled down to 40 and dropping.

By the time Eric told me what was happening, his serotonin levels were far below normal. He confided in me that he was so depressed that sleeping all afternoon was the only way he could restore his emotional energy. His wife, Laura, was barely holding it together, constantly on the verge of tears.

Upon hearing his story, I prayed for Eric, but I was his biggest advocate to quit. I've got to admit, I was upset with God on Eric's behalf. I saw what was happening to his family and couldn't bear to see him go on. He had come to realize that he couldn't sustain this kind of life but needed permission to walk away. His biggest question was, "What will people think of me?"

A Liberating Discovery

As church planters we're not trained to give up easily. We're conditioned to endure any and all struggles in the name of faithfulness. But this is not what God intended. No one ever tells us that Jesus made church planting the only endeavor with an exit strategy.

Let's go back to the story of Jesus sending his disciples to villages, looking for persons of peace in Matthew 10:14: "If anyone will not welcome you or listen to your words, shake the dust off your feet when you leave that house or town."

In other words, if people don't respond to the gospel and if your ministry is not being received, you're not obligated to stick around. Go ahead, move on. You've done your job. It may not have been to plant a church, but it still accomplished Christ's mission. What a liberating realization!

Leaving your mission field does not mean you've missed God's calling or that you've wasted years of your life. You may have paved the way for another church planter to continue the mission. Like a relay race handoff, you cultivated the community far enough for the next pastor to step in. You made it that much easier for him, and only you could have done this.

Or there might be another explanation altogether.

The Jeremiah Calling

God's purpose in sending you to plant a church might not have been to plant a church at all.

I remember sitting in tears at a Willow Creek conference back in 2002, listening to Bill Hybels describe "the Jeremiah calling." This is where God sends you as an ambassador to offer one more grace-filled invitation to a hard-hearted community. Unfortunately it's the ministry of unfruitful evangelism, and new churches don't usually come out of it. But nonetheless, it's in the nature of God to be long-suffering in his compassion for the lost.

For a solid three years in Reston, I thought this was my calling.

As it turns out, God planted an amazing church there. But the truth is God doesn't need us to plant thriving churches. That's not the end-all, be-all of his mission. Glorifying himself is the chief end of his activities, and sometimes our fruitless struggle best serves this cause. If only we could settle for this end. Our lives as church planters would be so much easier. Just know that the Word of God will not return void. None of our kingdom efforts are wasted.

Shake the Dust off Your Feet

The Bible is filled with stories that give us permission to leave infertile places. The common refrain "shake the dust off your feet" signifies that we are to leave bad soil behind.

In Pisidian Antioch, Paul and Barnabas found Jewish leaders who opposed the gospel and began stirring up persecution. Their response in Acts 13:49–51 was to leave town:

> The message of the Lord spread through the whole
> region. But the Jews incited the religious women of
> high standing and the leading men of the city. They
> stirred up persecution against Paul and Barnabas and
> expelled them from their district. But shaking the dust
> off their feet against them, they proceeded to Iconium.

In other places, Paul found good ground and stayed longer to cultivate the soil. Look at 1 Corinthians 16:8–9: "But I will stay in Ephesus until Pentecost, because a wide door for effective ministry has opened for me—yet many oppose me."

Jesus did the same thing. He longed for people to embrace him as Savior, but he moved on if the area was infertile. Take, for instance, his hometown of Nazareth, which was a bit thorny, as we see in Matthew 13:54–58:

He went to His hometown and began to teach them in their synagogue, so that they were astonished and said, "How did this wisdom and these miracles come to Him? Isn't this the carpenter's son? Isn't His mother called Mary, and His brothers James, Joseph, Simon, and Judas? And His sisters, aren't they all with us? So where does He get all these things?" And they were offended by Him.

But Jesus said to them, "A prophet is not without honor except in his hometown and in his household." And He did not do many miracles there because of their unbelief.

Jesus was constantly performing soil tests to determine where he should minister. If it was good ground, he stayed. If it was bad ground, he moved on.

Be Smart about It

In the same passage where Jesus instructs his disciples to look for spiritual fertility, he cautions them to be as peaceful as doves but as shrewd as snakes. He wanted them to be smart about their ministries and not be destroyed by tough soil.

He was giving them permission to walk away when they faced impenetrable resistance, knowing full well that their mission was accomplished.

In the words of Kenny Rogers, "You've got to know when to hold 'em, know when to fold 'em, know when to walk away, and know when to run."

Jesus wanted us to watch for signs of spiritual fertility and adapt our ministry strategies to accommodate them. Few church planters consider the spiritual fertility of their communities, and I want to help change that.

Saying Good-bye

In February 2008 I said good-bye to the congregation I had founded and cultivated for the past seven years. It was the most difficult decision I'd ever made because so much of my heart was invested in that church. The decision was a surprise to everyone, but somehow God had prepared their hearts for the handoff to my good friend and associate pastor. We shared tears, but we also had a sense of agreement that God was in this.

The spiritual infertility of our community had brought tremendous heaviness to my heart over the years. If only I had known that church planting wasn't supposed to feel like that, I could have experienced so much more joy.

I realized at the end of my journey that God had called me to be a cultivator. He used Ainsley and me to nurture relationships that would provide a fertile seedbed for a church plant to come. To this day Reston Community Church is thriving and growing as they build on that foundation.

Leave with This

As a church planter, you are one of God's choice servants. He loves you, he cares for you, and he doesn't want you to fail. Put your hand to the plow or grab your sickle. Know the condition of the soil beneath your feet. And prepare for the harvest that God wants to gather through your ministry.

QUESTIONS FROM PART 1

Tough Soil

1. What are the struggles your church plant is facing?
2. How have you been trying to resolve these issues until now?
3. Could you see how infertile soil might be causing some of them?
4. Have there been other struggling church plants in your area?
5. Have you thought about giving up? What keeps you there?

Challenge: Write down all of the outreaches you've conducted in your community. Note which ones have truly made an impact.

Spiritual Fertility

1. On a scale of 1 to 10 (10 being strongest), how would you rate the spiritual receptivity of your community?
2. What signs of spiritual fertility do you see?

3. What signs of spiritual infertility do you see?
4. In what ways are people practically asking for a church?
5. What communities do you know of that have a dormant spiritual heritage?

Challenge: Talk to some local, established pastors in your target community. Ask them to tell you about the area's spiritual receptivity.

Cultivation

1. Which of your activities fall under the category of building an organization?
2. Which activities could be classified as cultivation?
3. Is your predominant activity the right fit for your community?
4. Do you feel pressure to get an organization off the ground?
5. How can you cultivate friendships without building an organization for now?

Challenge: Begin a friendship with someone who is not a Christ follower without the motive of assimilating him or her into your church.

People of Peace

1. What needs do you have that could be met by a person of peace?
2. Where might you find God-fearing people in your community?
3. Name one or more persons of peace in your life.
4. Which nonbelievers fall under this category?

5. How have these people impacted your ministry so far?

Challenge: Write thank-you notes to the individuals who have paved the way for your church. Tell them about the Matthew 10 principle and how God has used them in your life.

Exit Strategy

1. Can you point to any persons of peace as an affirmation of your calling?
2. Is church planting having devastating effects on you or your family?
3. What conditions must be in place for you to walk away?
4. Do you struggle with guilt over the prospect of moving on?
5. What other purposes has God fulfilled through you besides establishing a church?

Challenge: Invite several pastors to conduct a spiritual health checkup on you and your church. If you don't know any, find some objective believers who will care for you, but also ask you hard questions.

Part 2

ROLLING ROCKS

6

NO MO

When Momentum Eludes You

Not long ago I came across the Web site of a local church that seemed new by all appearances. The graphics were edgy, they met in a portable environment, and the pastor had a blog. What more screams church plant? And because Ainsley and I had sworn off megachurches in favor of a start-up, we decided to check it out.

As we pulled into the parking lot five minutes before service time, I could tell they were struggling. First, ours was only the fourth car in the parking lot. And second, the greeter at the front door stared at us like he'd never seen a visitor before. Still, I'm a church planter at heart so a few awkward moments aren't enough to deter me. I've had my fair share of difficult Sunday mornings.

As we entered the building, which was a day care facility during the day, the people were friendly enough. By the way, every church thinks they're friendly. (They're not.) And every friendly church mistakenly thinks that's enough to help them succeed. (It's not.)

But as we entered the makeshift auditorium, there were only six of us in the service. And I'm not positive about this, but I think the other two couples were related to each other. Yowzer.

Granted, it was Memorial Day weekend, and the pastor, who also led worship that morning, was apologetic about the absentees. Usually the crowd was bigger, he confessed. I wondered if attendance was down 50 percent or maybe 100 percent. Truth is, it didn't matter. It would have taken a 1,000 percent increase to feel even the slightest bit comfortable in that room. My heart bled for this guy. I felt the weight of discouragement and embarrassment he must have been experiencing.

For his sake I was glad we were there. And it was obvious that the other two couples were glad we were there too. After the service was over, we braced ourselves for an interrogation. *Were we from the area? How long had we been living here? Oh, we just moved here? Would we take the leftover doughnuts home with us?* I could sense their hope. They were practically salivating over us. A "normal family" is like a golden chalice for every church planter.

Their hope was futile. I wanted to encourage the group. I wanted to hug them all and tell them how remarkable they were. I wanted to tell them to keep up the good work. But there was no chance we were coming back. There were so many problems; I couldn't even begin to tell you. But I was curious. I had to know what was going on, the backstory.

Having been a church planter, I knew to never ask about numbers. That's an offensive tactic. If someone wants to offer up that information, he'll do it on his own volition. But there are more encouraging questions to ask. No church planter is doing as well as he'd like, and he doesn't want a nosy outsider's selfish curiosity to be served.

So I asked the planter, "How long have you been meeting?"

I thought this question would give him a way to justify the hardship. New churches certainly aren't expected to run large numbers. They're fueled by hope, by what's ahead of them. And from what I could tell, this church couldn't have been more than a few weeks old. It was my way of supporting him with an encouraging question. I was setting him up with a good excuse. But his answer shocked me.

"Eight years," he said.

If I had been drinking coffee, I would have spewed it all over myself. I had to ask for clarification because I couldn't believe my ears. How in the world this guy made it eight years had to be some kind of phenomenon. To push ahead year after year with fewer than twenty people—no, fewer than twelve people—was mind-blowing. And what's remarkable is this fellow showed no signs of slowing down. He was rallying people for a water bottle giveaway that next weekend at the community fair. He was promoting his sermon podcasts on the Web, for crying out loud.

I think he honestly believed his big breakthrough was right around the corner. My heart still aches just thinking about him. I'm not saying he won't make it. You never know. But this guy's experience is not unlike that of thousands and thousands of church planters who charge straight for the gates of hell, only to fall flat on their backs and never know what hit them.

All of their passionate idealism turns into one big glorious letdown.

The Glorious Letdown

Church planters are born with a strong dose of idealism. Like a polar bear needs a good, thick coat of fur, church planters need idealism to survive. It takes every ounce of faith and courage to get a new church off the ground. That's not to say they have to be fearless. Quitting a job and moving to a new town to launch a church is terrifying. But I've never met a church planter who didn't think they could do it. I believe God hardwires this naïveté into us. Otherwise, we might never take the leap of faith into this grand adventure.

No one else but a church planter would ever move to a new city with no contacts, no history, and no promise of success. It's a holy naïveté that drives us to attempt the impossible. Not long ago I got an e-mail from a young guy who was thinking of moving his family to Arizona from central Tennessee to start a new church.

I thought for a moment then typed back, "Do you know anyone in Arizona?"

He responded a few seconds later: "No, do you?"

Like I said, no one but a church planter.

Divine Naïveté

Idealism in a church planter is like the forgetfulness of labor pains by a mother. After Ainsley spent nineteen hours in natural labor with our son Wyatt, I thought, *Well, she'll never do that again.* But two years later my wife insisted on delivering our second son Dylan naturally as well. Me? I spent most of those eight hours just trying to stay vertical.

This maternal forgetfulness is God given. John 16:21 confirms it: "When a woman is in labor she has pain because her time has come. But when she has given birth to a child, she no longer remembers the suffering because of the joy that a person has been born into the world."

I'm convinced that church planters are endowed with a divine spirit of idealism. And rightfully so. If they knew exactly what they were in for, they might never do it. But when this idealism becomes the voice of reason for the planter, it can create a ton of problems. It leads to a church without momentum. And there's nothing more destructive to a church planter's well-being than starting a church with no momentum.

A Different Kind of Church Plant

I marvel at how church planters will elevate the heroes of church planting, read their blogs, buy their books, and attend their conferences, but start their churches in the exact opposite way. They embrace these leaders' spirit of faith and determination but completely neglect their strategies—all because of idealism. And this creates a different kind of church plant.

It's a church that's started from scratch. A parachute-drop plant. A church against all odds. A church that's sprouted from nothing. And no momentum.

Have you ever seen one of those nature shows that documents a baby sea turtle's journey to life? The mother lays hundreds of eggs in the sand and then leaves them buried while they gestate. Meanwhile, all the local snakes come by to wait for dinner. When the babies are finally born, they make a mad dash for the water before they're eaten alive. They certainly weren't set up for success by their mother.

That's like a church plant launched out of idealism. You hope they make it, but they're not exactly set up for success. The snakes in the grass are lying in wait. Until these baby congregations can reach critical mass, they face a number of daunting challenges. Here are a few of them:

Always an Outsider

A church that's not birthed out of an indigenous movement will always be perceived as an outsider to the local population. Every community is different, and churches that aren't local simply aren't trusted. Years pass before the planter can gain acceptance or even begin to think like a local.

Financially Dependent

A church planter starting from scratch has to figure out a financial model to survive—whether it's bivocational ministry, outside support, or local tithes. If he depends on the young congregation for financial support, he puts tremendous pressure on them. If they don't step up to the challenge, the planter often gets frustrated with them, and they grow resentful. God certainly doesn't want people to pay for the cost of their own salvation.

Stretched Thin

A new church relies heavily on volunteers to carry the load of ministry. And by God's grace, he sends us servant-hearted people to get the job done. But a church without momentum unloads the organizational workload onto these people and never takes it off. They serve every week, often without breaks, and they can't ever step down without appearing unspiritual.

A Charity in and of Itself

People want a church with vision that's bigger than they are. They want to join a church that's leveraging its influence and resources to change the world. Churches without momentum become a charity in and of themselves. The planter spends most of his time begging people to help improve the church. The mission and the message are largely focused on the church's survival.

Prematurely Launched

When church planters get a vision for a new congregation, few of them wait for the right time to launch it. Most planters launch too quickly, which is a setup for failure. They have a field of dreams philosophy that says, "If you start it, they will come." But nothing could be further from the truth. A church plant's success is directly the result of everything that went into it before it launched. In other words, the better you prepare, the better the church plant.

A Church with Momentum

John Maxwell is famous for his sixteenth irrefutable law of leadership called the law of the big mo. This law states that leaders create forward motion in an organization by achieving and nurturing small victories. I love how John made momentum sound so fun and personal by calling it "Mo." I've heard him do this with Jesus' disciples too: Pete, Jim, and John.

And it's true. When your church plant reaches critical mass, Mo is indeed your best friend. People hear about your church through word of mouth, large donors call you because they can't think of a better recipient, influential people are attracted to the movement that is your church, and good things start to happen. And you can't control it. Momentum can't be put into a formula or bottled. You just know when you have it. It's an invisible force that makes everything come easily.

But what Maxwell didn't say is that unless you already have Mo, it doesn't want to be your friend. It tries to reject and elude you. It doesn't want you to achieve it. And a church plant without momentum simply cannot win. The planter takes two steps forward and three steps back. Just when giving is up, attendance is down. The same week a new guest comes to visit, all of your core families are gone. The sound system didn't work. The video projector was down.

Church planters in these circumstances have a ready list of "if only" items that would help them reach critical mass:

- If only everyone would attend on the same Sunday.
- If only giving would increase by $1,000 a week.
- If only the high school location would come available.
- If only we had five more small group leaders.

But these "if only" conditions are fleeting. They're like scared squirrels. Just when you think you can get them to eat off your hand, they run away from you.

In his best-selling book *Good to Great*, Jim Collins likens momentum to a giant, concrete flywheel that will start to spin if you just push long and hard enough. It's possible that this book added years to my personal threshold for perseverance. But what Collins didn't say is that the giant, concrete flywheel of momentum has a tension wire that pulls backward and has large, sharp spikes that swing back and hurt you.

No Mo Will Hurt You

In part 1 of this book, I told the story of how I tried hosting a Maximum Impact simulcast to reach business leaders in our community and only eight people showed up. For months leading up to that event, I spent every waking hour trying to drum up interest. Real estate offices, mortgage firms, the health club—I tried everyone to no avail. But then I discovered gold when I came across a Christian businessmen's Bible study that met every Tuesday morning at 7:00 a.m. They

were community leaders, Christians; and they liked John
Maxwell. Bingo.

I attended the Bible study for months, preparing to
extend an invitation. I didn't want to appear opportunistic.
But I was a parachute-drop church planter, and I was desper-
ate. As the event drew closer, I looked for a strategic entry
point. I noticed that the Bible study leader, a financial planner by day, welcomed announcements from the group before
concluding with prayer every week. It was my window of
opportunity.

I carefully rehearsed my speech, which announced that
John Maxwell and Lou Holtz were going to appear live on
screen at the Reston Sheraton ballroom for just $40 a person
and free breakfast. What a great opportunity to invite
unchurched coworkers to a high-quality business event at a
local church.

Two weeks out I mustered enough courage to make the
announcement. I knew I was an outcast in the group. I was a
young pastor; they were older, successful businessmen. Still
I thought they had grown to like me and accept me. Some
had even invited me to lunch, although it might have been
to sell me insurance. But I thought I had a grace-filled room.
I felt like I had a clean shot.

As soon as I finished my announcement, a contractor on
the other side of the room barked that his church was also
hosting the simulcast—for free. Another businessman piped
in from across the room, "Free? Now that's my kind of event.
I'm going to that one." The whole room murmured with
approval. Someone mocked, "Yeah, why would I pay $40
when I can get it for free? Har, har, har, har."

My heart sank like a lead balloon. As soon as the Bible
study was over, I made a beeline for the parking lot and never
went back. I desperately needed these men's involvement in

the event, but they lunged at me like snakes at a baby sea turtle. All of these guys knew my plight. They knew I was a struggling church planter trying to make it in a big town. But I had no mo going for me. And no matter how God-honoring my endeavor was, nobody likes a loser. Everyone likes a winner. When it comes to momentum, the "have nots" keep losing, and the "haves" continue to get more and more.

I'm just going to say it. That experience wounded me. And it wasn't the only discouraging encounter. I could tell you story after story of how fighting for momentum left me limping. And so could every church planter who has tried to start without it. There is a formula for enduring as a church planter that looks something like this:

Faith > Wounds = We endure.

Faith < Wounds = We quit.

As long as our faith is greater than our wounds, we can hold out. But if the scale is tipped and our wounds become too great, we start to deconstruct. This is where sin, depression, and anger start to creep into our lives.

Wounded church planters don't realize it at first. They go through a process of analyzing their circumstances, but they hardly ever recognize lack of momentum as the culprit. I've never heard a church planter confess that he launched without momentum. They think that's just the way it's supposed to be. It's supposed to be hard. It's supposed to be nearly impossible. Yet momentum is a critical factor of success for a church in the making.

Here are the four phases of rationalization that a struggling planter goes through:

Year 1: "We used the wrong outreach tactics, but now we know better."

Year 2: "We didn't understand the community, but now we're a part of it."

Year 3: "My people don't get the vision. It's their fault."

Year 4: "Maybe it's me. Maybe I should quit."

Sadly the church planter is off base with every one of these diagnoses.

They never see it as a momentum issue. And by the time they reach year four, they're looking for a way out. They're looking for jobs online, testing the waters for a nice staff job at another church, and spending less time in outreach and sermon prep as the ministry slows to a crawl.

And sometimes it's worse. I once heard Mark Driscoll say that adultery rates for pastors are so high because they're trying to get away from the wounds of ministry and don't know a better way. They essentially hit the "eject button." I've never done this, but I can understand it. No Mo has kicked my tail a time or two.

The plight of every church planter is to push long and hard enough against the giant, concrete flywheel until it starts spinning on its own. The goal is to create momentum. But the trouble is, you can't. At least, not without injuring yourself or the church plant. It's the great deception of every church planter that you can manufacture momentum on your own. You can only identify it. And if it invites you in, you can join it.

Let me tell you how.

7

MOMENTUM-BASED CHURCH PLANTING

The Backstory of a Movement

Several years after launching my church, a popular area director for Young Life also decided to start a church in Charlottesville, Virginia. He had been a youth leader in that area for years and had impacted untold numbers of teenagers for Christ. But even more, he had a personal charisma that made him the center of every room he entered. He seemed to know everyone in town, and everyone knew him. His likability factor was off the charts.

For someone like me, who had worked extremely hard to launch a new congregation, what I saw him do was nothing short of remarkable. Within just a few months, he had attracted hundreds of people to his new church. People were meeting God. The church was exploding. It became a spiritual movement in Charlottesville, which had historically not received new churches very well.

Now I'm all for the kingdom of God, but I have to admit that I was pretty frustrated by what I saw. Why couldn't my church plant do that? From all outside appearances, this planter was a prodigy. It was easy to point to his talent or his charisma as the reason for his success. He was an excellent communicator. He had a great worship band. He was in a college town. He prayed a lot. Maybe that was the reason.

But I couldn't dismiss his success so easily. I've met too many church planters who were just as talented, charming, and prayerful that never made it.

Here's a bit of insider info. When this church planter launched his church, there was a ready-made congregation of people who had respected him, trusted him, and followed his leading for the past ten years. These were former Young Life kids who were now grown up and raising children of their own. They were college students who had seen the impact of this man's life and fallen in love with his charisma. They were friends who had benefited from his companionship and guidance for years. When he planted the church, it was like exposing a keg of gunpowder to a spark. His church plant catalyzed his social network.

Church as a Social Movement

Planting churches is not just a spiritual endeavor. It is a social movement. Or in many cases the lack of one.

When I take my kids to the beach, we love to build trenches in the sand and watch the waves fill them with water. What's fun is that we can make these moats into any shape we like. We can create a circular trench around a castle. We can write our names. We can do whatever we like. But unless we build a trench, the water disappears into the sand. By digging patterns, we're giving the water a channel to follow, a holding place. We're telling it which way to go so that it will fill our moats.

Social networks are like trenches in the sand. By building relationships before we plant a church, we are creating channels for the gospel to fill. And if we don't build them, the gospel will have no impact. It will disappear into the sand.

Here's the honest truth: when you're starting out, people don't care about your church. If they care about anything, they care about you, and, more specifically, whether you care about them. This becomes the foundation for your church plant and for the gospel to have impact.

Struggling churches aren't always spiritual casualties. Sometimes they're failed social movements. The planter simply didn't build enough trenches.

The Movement of the Gospel

I'd feel guilty for offering this theory if it weren't so biblical. When you read the book of Acts, you can clearly see how God used social networks to carry his gospel throughout the ancient world like a trench carries water.

In Acts 2:5, God had drawn Jews "from every nation under heaven" to one place, at one time, for one God-appointed meeting. It was the feast of Pentecost, and every God-fearing Jew was required to attend. They spoke different languages. They smelled of different spices. Every culture was represented. It was the prime opportunity for a revelation that could be carried back to their hometowns . . . like water through a trench. These Jews didn't know it, but God had appointed them as carriers of a sort of spiritual virus that would take the gospel to faraway places. Believe it or not, that wasn't coincidental.

When we fail to dig our own trenches (in other words, if we fail to build relationships), God takes matters into his own hands. His gospel depends on a social network to carry it. It's like a tick waiting on a leaf for a deer to pass by. A barnacle waiting for a ship. This is why the command to "make disciples" is inextricably linked to the word *go*. The gospel requires movement.

Burn

God wants his followers to create social movements so that the gospel can spread. Ultimately a new church's purpose is not to become a congregation; it's to manifest the glory of God. The more churches there are, the more glory. So if we don't create movement, he'll do it for us. Watch what he did in Acts 8:1: "On that day a severe persecution broke out against the church in Jerusalem, and all except the apostles were scattered throughout the land of Judea and Samaria."

Look at that. God cares so much about spreading the gospel through social networks that he'll use any means necessary to get us to move. Even if it means persecution.

Have you ever seen a movie where the villain thinks he's safe from a fire he started . . . until he notices the trail of gasoline leading to his own feet? Jesus essentially lit his followers on fire so they'd run like mad for the outlying areas. And when they did, they carried the gospel with them.

In Acts 1:8, Jesus predicted that his followers would take the gospel to Judea and Samaria. But they seemed to have trouble getting there on their own. So he essentially doused his followers with gasoline and then set Jerusalem on fire. He watched them burn with passion and spread his message as they went. Acts 8:4 tells us that "those who had been scattered preached the word wherever they went" (NIV).

On This Rock

Church planters tend to ignore entire passages of Scripture in favor of their own theories and models. Matthew 16:18 is one of them: "And I also say to you that you are Peter, and on this rock I will build My church, and the forces of Hades will not overpower it."

I once learned in a childbirth class that a pregnant woman's uterus is so powerful it will push out the baby on its own, even if the mother doesn't do it. The same is true of the church. Even if we don't intend to start new churches, God will see that his church is multiplied.

God will build his own church. Not just the megachurch down the street. Not just the talented leader's church that has a great worship band and prays a lot. And not the universal church at the exclusion of yours. God will build *his* church. And that includes your church plant. God cares deeply about the growth and the multiplication of his church, and your new congregation is a part of his plan.

God builds his church by creating social networks around you. He brings you into contact with people and circumstances that contribute to a thriving congregation. By ignoring this divine field positioning, we miss out on the church God has been building around us all this time. Do you see why starting from scratch is not only unnecessary but also ridiculous? We're turning our backs on the assistance that God has willingly provided.

Let me ask you this: What social network has God been building around you to become his church? What people has he put in your life? How many people know that you care about them? What community has your influence created? What trenches have you been digging? Where do you see a church in the making?

If this network doesn't exist, I would dare say it's not time to plant a church. It's time to build some trenches. Time to create a network.

If we truly believed that God builds his church, it would radically change the way we start new churches. Most of us are guilty of trying to initiate the work of God rather than join it. We try to launch new congregations without first building relationships with people. God plants his church on the rock of the gospel, but it's a rock that needs movement.

It's a rolling rock.

A Cause Laid upon a Movement

When a church plant grows quickly, it's usually because of the relational network that preceded it. Nothing travels as fast as a powerful cause that's laid upon a social movement. It's like a baseball that's loaded into a pitching machine. It goes from zero to ninety mph in a short time.

How many times have you heard the familiar story of a popular youth pastor who decided to plant in the same town and ended up with a megachurch on his hands? This wasn't just an overnight sensation or a spontaneous move of God. It was the result of God's building his church for years and years through this leader's ministry.

Accidental Momentum

The first time I tapped into a social movement was completely by accident. I was working as a copywriter at an advertising agency in Ohio after college but wanted to help my father's struggling, rural church make a bigger impact. There were only five kids in the youth group, and I thought this might be the most natural way to help.

Rather than starting a small group for these five teenagers, which would have been the logical first step, I decided to go after a more audacious goal. I asked the owner of an old theater on Main Street if I could rent his facility on Saturday nights throughout the summer to host a series of youth outreach events. I offered him all the money from concessions if he'd let me use the place for free. The building had been converted from a nineteenth-century gristmill into a meeting hall that was mostly used for banjo concerts and polka dances. The owner was thrilled to have us. My only challenge was to fill the place, and unfortunately I didn't know any other teenagers.

What I didn't realize, however, was that the teenagers in our small town were a social movement waiting for a cause. They were bored. They were broke. And there was nothing more exciting to do than smoke cigarettes and grope each other in the Wal-Mart parking lot.

Now I need to point out that I had nothing to do with creating this movement. It already existed. These kids were like gunpowder to the small spark I was about to light. It was a revolution in the making. All it took was five teenagers to start talking to their friends about an exciting event, and the news spread like wildfire.

On opening night more than 125 kids packed into that old theater, and we never looked back. I hired several youth bands to play onstage, asked my friends to star in some irreverent skits, and purchased a few prizes with my meager copywriter's salary to offer as giveaways. On the first night I gave my best evangelistic message without ever having preached before, and five kids decided to trust in Jesus. It was one of the most thrilling summers of my life. I had unknowingly tapped into a network. I had laid a cause upon a movement.

Spotting a Movement

Church planters are great at promoting causes—the cause of the gospel, the cause of a new church, and the cause of reaching lost people. But most of us are bad at spotting movements. It's the shortsightedness of our God-given idealism. We try to use the gospel to create movement, but it just doesn't work. We try to lead people with vision, but our fresh, new approach doesn't seem to impress anyone. Without relationship, people don't care about the gospel. And they certainly don't care about your church.

Let me say that again: people don't care about your church.

The people in your community don't have time to sift through all the new churches clamoring for attention in your area to find the right one for them. So they listen to their friends. They watch where everyone else is going and join them. It doesn't matter how good your service, your worship, or your preaching is, your church is ultimately judged by social network.

The winning churches keep winning. They keep attracting people and growing larger, while the losing churches keep losing. It's the way of the social economy. In fact, the winning churches can have services that are lacking, but the sheer number of people in attendance will make them attractive.

Buzz covers a multitude of sins.

The losing churches, on the other hand, are doomed to face setback after setback until they achieve critical mass, which is almost never. Visitors will always feel awkward and skeptical in these environments until there's a sufficient level of social validation.

I'm convinced that when God calls a planter to start a church, he calls him either to start a social network first (which can take years) or simply to leverage the one he's been building around him. Sometimes a planter feels like he can't start a church in his own community because of his senior pastor's resistance or the fear of oversaturating a community. But walking away from a movement that God has been nurturing around you for years is even more tragic. Bringing together a social network is one of the first things God does to create a church in the making. If he's building his church, he won't let a resistant senior pastor get in the way of it. In fact, God might change that pastor's heart.

A Church That Was Waiting to Happen

One of my good friends, Mike McKinley, served on staff at Capitol Hill Baptist Church in Washington, DC, several years ago. The senior pastor, Dr. Mark Dever, is intelligent, highly accomplished, and loaded with charisma. People drive for hours to attend his standing-room-only services. But he also places a high priority on training other pastors and empowering them to lead their own churches.

When my friend Mike felt called to revitalize an old, dying church called Guilford Baptist, Capitol Hill got behind him. They trained him in spiritual leadership, gave him opportunities to preach, offered him start-up funds, and encouraged people in the church to join him. They decided to use their powerful social network to launch a church with momentum.

Incidentally, I was part of an assessment team that evaluated Guilford Baptist before Mike got there. Our conclusion was that it was a lost cause. It was as dead as a doornail.

At first only a handful of people decided to join Mike, perhaps too cautious to leave their beloved home church behind. But within the next two years, Mike's church quickly swelled to maximum seating capacity. His expositional preaching and conservative approach to church attracted people who were driving long distances to attend Capitol Hill Baptist. A homeschooling network spread the news about Guilford's kindred approach to teaching children. And students from a local Christian college resonated with Mike's teaching. When I visited Guilford Baptist, I saw a congregation that was made up of people who fit well together.

Mike had found the perfect combination of cause and social network. It was the right mix for what his community needed. And he couldn't have done it without the network of his mother church. He launched out of the momentum of Capitol Hill Baptist and easily broke through the barrier of critical mass. Mike even turned down additional sponsorship money in year two because they were doing so well.

How to Launch a Church

Once you've been a part of a movement, you'll never do it any other way. After you've witnessed the ease and thrill of seeing a movement carry a cause, you'll never tolerate the agonizing challenge of starting a church from scratch. Every parachute-drop planter I've met would go back and do it differently if he could.

I'm a passionate proponent of momentum-based church planting. This is where you start with a team, funding, leadership, and a social network. Sometimes God calls us to build these conditions first, which can delay the start of our churches. But if we launch out before the movement is ready, we'll have an extraordinarily difficult time reaching critical mass. We'll put our congregations in a vulnerable position from day one. And once we launch, we can never go back to the spirit of hope and anticipation that comes from new beginnings.

God builds his church by creating momentum. To plant from scratch is to disregard the circumstances and relationships God has been shaping around us for years. There's no reason to do it alone. God doesn't send us out to the front lines with the promise of waiting until you get back. Rather, God will move heaven and earth to build his church. The gates of hell will not prevail against it. But first you have to know how God creates a movement.

You have to know how a crowd comes together.

8

THE ANATOMY OF A CROWD

Finding the Key to a Culture

In my first staff job as a collegiate pastor, I was asked to chaperone a weeklong youth mission trip to Budapest, Hungary. What I thought would be a cushy job of hiking through Europe and consoling homesick junior high students turned out to be one of the most frustrating experiences of my life.

This wasn't your typical mission trip. It was a street drama team. And in some freak twist of happenstances, I ended up as the central character in this production. Basically it was an allegory of the gospel. An evil villain lures a town of villagers into captivity and laughs at their misery. My character, the young prince, arrives in heroic fashion to battle the antagonist but ends up offering his own life in exchange for the others. He rises from the dead to free the prisoners, and a celebration ensues.

While we performed this spectacle on sidewalks, town squares, and parking lots, a Hungarian sound track narrated the events in dramatic tones. There were sword fights with

PVC pipes, and all of us wore black pants, white T-shirts, and blue vests. We looked like circus freaks. But the twelve junior high students and I gave our all every single day. We each took turns giving our testimony after the play while the rest of the team handed out tracts.

There was only one problem. No one stopped to watch.

While performing in the middle of a village square, an angry café owner complained that we were disturbing his lunch guests. At a playground where we were performing for no one, a heckler pelted us with eggs from a sixth-story apartment balcony. The only real crowd was inside Slovakia where we performed for a band of Gypsies. They stank like eggs and yelled at us through their sparse, rotting teeth. It was a miserable experience. At the end of a long week, we were grateful to spend our final day shopping in downtown Budapest.

As we walked through the beautiful streets of that ancient city, we came upon a large crowd of people gathered in a circle. They were laughing, cheering, and straining to see through the people in front of them. We inched closer to the crowd to see what was going on and heard the sound of an American hip-hop song that was popular in the early 1990s. We stood on our tiptoes to see what was going on and were shocked to see break-dancers.

They had laid pieces of cardboard across the hard, cobblestone street and were popping and locking their way into the crowd's affections. Even their clothes were comical. One leg of their sweatpants was pulled up to their knees; some wore beanies to protect their hair during head spins. People were throwing money into a tip jar and eating up every moment of it. Within minutes the Budapest police raced onto the scene and broke up the party.

As our team walked away, I couldn't help but wonder if we'd picked the wrong way to attract a crowd.

Making Multitudes

Crowds don't come together easily. Just ask the local restaurant owner, the event planner, and especially the church planter. There has to be a popular cause, a recognized need, or a personal connection. A crowd doesn't come together unless there are enough people who share the same preferences. And there must be a way for them to communicate with one another for the idea to spread.

John 12:32 teaches that God draws all people to himself. I've seen him arrange people and circumstances in such a way that his long-lost children will find him. But thousands of church planters have never experienced this reality. And what for them? That's my question. What for those who preach the gospel and pray faithfully but never see their church plants grow?

Sociology can be just as important to a church planter's plight as theology. If we can't gather a crowd, then the gospel seeds have nowhere to grow. I know plenty of pastors who believe that the mere presence of a crowd is the sign of a compromised gospel. But the greatest movements of God, the greatest revivals, have happened among crowds.

Just look at Billy Graham. Before he traveled to California for the now-famous Los Angeles crusades, newspaper mogul William Randolph Hearst wired his west coast office with the instructions to "puff Graham." That single telegram catalyzed a crowd of unprecedented sizes. And Hearst wasn't even a believer. Keep in mind that what drew people to Graham was not initially his spiritual content. It was his charisma, his authoritative figure, and his connection to celebrities. He was larger than life. Hollywood begged him to appear in movies. The impact of his spiritual message goes without saying. But other factors got the crowd there.

Gathering a crowd is not a sin. I recently made the transition from being a church planter to an event producer. My job is to gather crowds. At first I wondered if making multitudes was OK. (You can take the pastor out of the church, but you can't take the guilt out of the pastor.) I've come to realize that gathering is a natural desire for people. We love to be around one another for the same purpose and experience.

Most church planters haven't figured out how to tap into this desire. If we could only figure out how to leverage human nature for righteous purposes, our ministry experiences would be radically different.

Jesus did.

When you look at Jesus' ministry, you see a remarkable knack for making multitudes. Just look at the stuff he used: the fish and loaves, the entertaining parables, the water to wine. Jesus even admitted that these activities were not always for spiritual purposes. When asked by his disciples why he spoke in confusing parables, he responded: "Though seeing, they do not see; though hearing, they do not hear or understand" (Matt. 13:13 NIV).

In other words, Jesus told parables to enlighten those who were seeking but simply to entertain those who were not. He knew that among the hundreds and thousands of people around him, most were not there for the right reason. But he welcomed them anyway. He loved them just the same. He knew that within the crowd were people who would become fully devoted to him. Jesus knew that disciple making was a numbers game. But he had to get the numbers; he had to draw the crowd.

Being OK with Wrong Motives

To gather a crowd requires a great tolerance for wrongly motivated people. It requires loving them anyway. When your church hosts an outreach event, people come for the free (fill in the blank). You've probably figured this out by now. You host a free movie night, buy down people's gas, or throw a cookout because you know that draws people. And you hope that out of the multitudes a few people will respond favorably to your church and maybe even the gospel. But the underlying principle is that you prey on people's greed and selfishness, albeit in small doses, to create an opportunity for the gospel.

The most effective churches have learned to do this on a large scale. At first these churches were viewed as heretical. They broke the religious rules that had been established for how to do church. But all they were doing was adapting their methods to make multitudes in a new era. Let me say it again: disciples come out of the multitudes.

Jesus never got angry with crowds for their wrong motives. He got angry with his disciples. He wept for the multitudes. But he never retaliated when people tried to take advantage of him. If Jesus ever had a good reason to raise his temper, it was on the cross. As he barely hung onto life, gasping for pockets of air, with blood pouring down his body, he looked at the mockers and curiosity seekers who had rejected him and prayed, "Father, forgive them, because they do not know what they are doing" (Luke 23:34).

Church planting is the fine art of emptying ourselves for people who reject us and forgiving them for the sake of the gospel.

blossins

Tapping into Needs

Something remarkable happened to me in 2008. I had been blogging for more than five years as a church planter and, without realizing it, had amassed a readership. Blogging brings the good and the bad into your life. You have a wider network of friends who encourage you and celebrate with you. But you also have a mob of critics who are ready to pounce on any grammatical oversight or differing opinion. For the most part, however, blogging has been a joy.

I decided in November 2008 that I wanted to host my own church leadership event. I had grown tired of traveling across the country to attend conferences, away from my wife and little boys. I hated flying, the impersonal hotel rooms, and the two- to three-day conference formats. So I thought I'd host an event in Reston, Virginia, my own backyard. I had just enough connections to invite eight relatively well-known speakers to my event. I asked them to speak for only thirty minutes and get to the point. I wanted one compelling idea, nothing more. I called it The Whiteboard Sessions.

What's incredible is that nearly nine hundred people wanted the same thing.

I didn't pay for a single advertisement or make one phone call to get anyone to come to the event. I simply blogged about it, e-mailed people, and encouraged the speakers to invite their own followings. It was a phenomenal success. As I mentioned, I now produce church leadership events for a living, but I've never seen an event publicized by word of mouth more than Whiteboard. Clearly I had scratched an itch. I had stumbled upon a desire that resonated with other leaders.

What Draws a Crowd

How did we in the church come to outlaw natural gifts that draw a crowd? Why do we quickly dismiss our natural abilities with spiritual explanations? Why do we act as though our talents are somehow sinful? The apostle Paul was humble. He had the cockiness beat out of him. But he didn't hesitate to roll out his credentials if anyone doubted his legitimacy.

Indeed, natural gifts are often the conduit God uses to gather an audience for his message. The miracles brought a platform for the truth. Raising the dead was actually pretty pointless considering the victims would die again later on, but it brought credibility to Jesus' message. We may not experience these crowd-builders today in quite the same way, but here are just a few of the conditions that make for a crowd:

Speaking Ability

God can choose to use anyone. Just look at Moses and Paul who both confessed their inadequacies at public speaking. But God does use our natural human strengths to further his kingdom.

The legendary preacher George Whitefield was famous for his ability to address thousands of people in outdoor preaching venues. His speaking ability was a social phenomenon. In fact, it prompted Benjamin Franklin to write this about him:

> He had a loud and clear voice, and articulated his
> words and sentences so perfectly, that he might be
> heard and understood at a great distance. . . . I had the
> curiosity to learn how far he could be heard, by
> [walking] backwards down the street towards the

river; and I found his voice distinct till I came near
Front-street, when some noise in that street obscured
it. Imagining then a semi-circle, of which my distance
should be the radius, and that it were filled with
[listeners], to each of whom I allowed two square feet,
I computed that he might well be heard by more than
thirty thousand.[1]

Think about that. Whitefield's voice was so powerful
that Benjamin Franklin spent the entire message trying to
calculate its reach.

Intelligence

God uses the intelligence of Al Mohler, president of Southern
Baptist Theological Seminary, to make multitudes. His mem-
ory is nearly photographic. I've heard that if you randomly
pull a book from the shelf of his vast library, he could tell
you the general content of the book without any prepara-
tion. Whenever I see Al being interviewed on CNN or other
news shows, it comforts me to know that he's representing
Christianity.

Family Connections

I used to watch Lakewood Church's pastor John Osteen on
TV until his untimely death on January 23, 1999. At this
time his family decided to continue the church's operations,
including the growing television ministry. As his son Joel
stepped into the preaching role, he had no experience, but
the church embraced him. He was a likable young man who
humbly stepped into his father's role. He captured the hearts
of Houston and millions of people who watch him on TV.
Today no American church even comes close to the size of
Lakewood's congregation.

Charisma

I spent a weekend with the staff of Capitol Hill Baptist Church in Washington, DC, where Dr. Mark Dever is pastor. I got to see a man whose quick wit and sharp intellect make him a larger-than-life figure. There was hardly an empty seat in his auditorium as close to a thousand young adults packed together tightly to hear him preach. Mark intentionally reads from a manuscript so that his personality doesn't take away people's focus from the Scriptures. By his own admission he has to harness his own gifts.

The Next Thing

Nothing draws more attention than something new and different. Ten years ago Perry Noble dreamed of starting a church that communicated the message of Jesus in the language of his culture. Born and bred in South Carolina, Perry was surrounded by traditional churches that clung to outdated, lifeless religion. When he started NewSpring Church, it changed the way a new generation saw God. Loud worship, edgy music, unabashed excellence, and humorous talks made for a highly impactful church experience. The church has grown to more than ten thousand people in just nine years.

Vision

Jerry Falwell had a vision to turn a mountainous town in rural Virginia into a global center for producing young champions for Christ. His vision was so clear and so defined that even my grandmother in Ohio wanted to be a part of it. She had a small piggy bank on her shelf that featured a photo of Liberty Mountain and the phrase "I want that mountain!" Today Jerry Falwell is no longer alive, but his vision still thrives. That mountain is now home to America's largest Christian university. I am a product of his ministry.

Find Your Gifting

Don't be discouraged by the level of giftedness that others possess. In some way, in some area, you are the best at what you do. It might take some deep introspection to figure out what that is. But it's in there. God gave you the capability to make crowds and to do it for his glory.

When I was a collegiate pastor, I offered to spend a day at the campus of any student who wanted me to visit. All went well until one particular girl asked me to come. She was the most socially awkward student in the bunch, and I wasn't exactly thrilled to tag along with her. I imagined us sitting by ourselves at a corner lunch table while the popular kids made fun of us. OK, I'm exaggerating slightly, but I prepared myself for an uncomfortable day. Imagine my surprise when I arrived on campus to discover that she was the leader of a substantial group of friends. They weren't the most popular kids in school, but they were smart; they were funny; and they could recite lines from any movie on cue.

I learned a valuable lesson that day. Everybody can lead somebody.

You are a level-10 leader in some way. It may not look like anyone else's gift, but God has equipped you with natural gifts that can make multitudes. The question is, do you use those gifts to point people to Jesus? I'm not trying to belittle the impact of the gospel, but many church planters lead only with the gospel and never find an audience. If you need someone to give you permission to hold off on the gospel until you draw a crowd, consider it granted.

The Crosshairs

For every endeavor there is a place where the crosshairs of your cause and the desires of other people come together. This is the place where a crowd is formed. But it might take some audacious risk-taking to find it. You might have to spend some time in R&D. You'll only get there by experiment. You have to be willing to screw up.

I wish I could've been in the same room with Joe Boyd when he came up with the idea for Aviator Church. It's a unique church in Derby, Kansas, that seeks to reach people employed in the airline industry. I can imagine the objections: "But what if someone doesn't work in the airline industry?" "That doesn't sound like a real church." "But there are no airplanes in the Bible."

We have to be willing to go where people are. It's their desires, their preferences that hold the secret to drawing a crowd. Most church planters start off with their own preferences, their own way of doing church; and consequently they have little success attracting people.

As church planters we have to be careful to plant the church our community needs, not the church in our heads.

Incarnating the Gospel

Meeting people where they're at is not as scandalous as you think. After all, Jesus came up with the idea. He was draped in glory with his Father in heaven when the rebellion of mankind delivered an affront to the holiness of God. We had made our own gods, went our own way in pride, and rejected the fellowship of God. But rather than consuming us with fire and starting over, Jesus became one of us. Look at this beautiful hymn from Philippians 2:5–8:

Let this mind be in you which was also in Christ Jesus,
who, being in the form of God, did not consider it
 robbery to be equal with God,
but made Himself of no reputation, taking the form of
 a bondservant, and coming in the likeness of men.
And being found in appearance as a man, He humbled
 Himself and became obedient to the point of
 death, even the death of the cross.

Jesus did not cling to his preferences. But out of love for us, out of the need to rescue us, he became a humble servant. He met us exactly where we were living.

This passage wouldn't disrupt our lives so much if it weren't for the first sentence: "Let this mind be in you." This statement is a charge to meet people where they are because we were once in the same position. We are to strip ourselves of our preferences and our identities and become like others for the sake of the gospel.

The first time I heard about XXX (triple-X) Church, which reaches out to men and women who are ensnared by lust at Las Vegas porn shows, it raised a big, red flag for me. *That's far too close to the enemy*, I thought. Those people don't even want to be rescued! But then I thought about Philippians 2:5–8. I was once the enemy of God. But Jesus came and met me on my level. I, too, didn't want to be delivered.

As a church planter, you need momentum to launch your church effectively. To achieve momentum you need a crowd. And to get a crowd, you have to meet people where they are. It's the point where your gifts and their desires come together. And guess what? You're allowed to do this. Who wants to plant a church for the already converted? It's more fun—not to mention, more worthwhile—to build an audience that has given you their trust and is open to the gospel you hope to deliver. It's better to reach people first. That is, if you know where to find them.

Let's go now to where the people can be found.

Notes

1. Benjamin Franklin quote taken from http://greatawakening documentary.com/items/show/23.

9

PEOPLE GROUPS

You'll Only Get So Far

The gospel can travel only so far before it reaches certain resistance. A church plant can only grow so large until it bumps into an invisible barrier. And, sadly, every church planter thinks his own leadership shortcomings are at fault. To be sure, the leadership revolution in the American church has spawned larger and larger congregations. But the truth is, not every church can reach every kind of person. There will always be unreachable people for every church plant because of its unique wiring and DNA. It takes all kinds of churches to reach all kinds of people. And the sooner we can embrace this fact, the sooner we can go after the people God has called us to reach.

These barriers to church growth are oftentimes cultural. There are subgroups of people within the greater population that come together based on all sorts of factors: affinity, shared interests, language, skin color, personality type, you name it. The most natural ones are ethnic, like Hispanic,

Chinese, and eastern European. But they can also be based on social class, geography, and even social health. (Can you think of a more bonded group of people than AA?) These are all subcultures that relate differently to one another, to the gospel, and, consequently, to your church plant. You simply cannot reach everyone. So it's important to understand the kind of people you can reach so that you can go about it more effectively.

Regardless of the type of culture, each group relates differently to the gospel, even in the subtlest ways. You would never expect a Kenyan congregation to show up on Sunday mornings in three-piece suits at a traditional, white clapboard building on the Serengeti Plain. Yet many church planters essentially do the same thing in their communities by misunderstanding cultural distinctives. Here are a few examples of cultural differences I've witnessed:

Blue Collar

Revolution Church in Canton, Georgia, is unapologetically reaching rednecks. They are being slightly facetious when they claim this because there are many highly educated people in the church. But they understand the unique blue-collar heritage of this community, and they planted a church that suits their interests. Revolution branded their church using strong black and red colors to appeal to men and regularly feature messages that address real issues of the working class.

Urban Artistic

Jumaine Jones is a Dallas Theological Seminary-trained church planter who understands the cultural distinctives of Silver Spring, Maryland—a metropolitan beltway community outside of Washington, DC. Before launching services for his new church, The Bridge, Jumaine hosted months of open mic nights at a local coffeehouse. The second event was standing room only as hundreds of aspiring poets, artists, and musicians came to showcase their talents. Jumaine's services on Sunday mornings reflect the same artistic flair, and the community is responding in a positive way.

Antiestablishment

Ron Jones is a former navy officer with a bleeding heart for marginalized young adults in downtown Norfolk, Virginia. He left a cushy staff job at a local megachurch to reach these left-lunging Bohemians with the mantra: "Love God. Love people. Prove it." His church, called Symphonic, holds services in a waterside warehouse that doubles as an art gallery and a concert venue for the downtown community. He's reaching people that would never step foot in a conventional church community.

Collegiate

Dave Proffitt is a natural with college students. He moved to Harrisonburg, Virginia, eight years ago to launch Aletheia Church on the campus of James Madison University. He and his wife, Shirley, moved into a house located just off campus so they could entertain the thousands of college students they interact with throughout the year. Dave's not afraid to share his life with them. In fact, he goes door-to-door every week because he knows college students are more open to conversations with a stranger than other communities might be. And it's paying off too. Aletheia Church just expanded to three other campuses, with plans of launching more. The Proffitts are now moving to Tampa, Florida, to reach college students with the same approach.

People Groups Were God's Idea

The subgroups that pose these cultural barriers to the gospel are called people groups, and all of them require a different approach to the gospel and a different form of church. I can imagine the arguments against this view. Yes, we must be true to the gospel, and there is clearly a biblical definition of church. We should not compromise either one. But by their very makeup, different people groups require different forms of church. I didn't come up with this idea. God is the one who created people groups. Just look at the story of the Tower of Babel in Genesis 11:1–7:

> At one time the whole earth had the same language and vocabulary. As people migrated from the east, they found a valley in the land of Shinar and settled there. . . .
>
> And they said, "Come, let us build ourselves a city and a tower with its top in the sky. Let us make a name for ourselves; otherwise, we will be scattered over the face of the whole earth."
>
> Then the LORD came down to look over the city and the tower that the men were building. The LORD said, "If, as one people all having the same language, they have begun to do this, then nothing they plan to do will be impossible for them. Come, let Us go down there and confuse their language so that they will not understand one another's speech."

God created cultural barriers by forming people groups to stop the rampant spread of sin. Without these barriers, without these cultural differences, sinfulness could spread quickly and easily like a virus. Think of people groups like a water bed. They're made up of separate water pockets so that if you accidentally cut open your mattress, you won't lose the entire water load on your bedroom floor. The barriers provide safety if something should go wrong.

The trouble is, when God created cultural barriers for sin, he effectively created cultural barriers for the gospel. Just as one manifestation of sin in Miami, Florida, has to get over the cultural barrier of Nashville, Tennessee, so the gospel has to get over the same cultural barriers.

This wasn't an oversight. Jesus didn't commission us to spread the gospel and start new churches with a blind eye to cultural barriers. He didn't mess up by trying to prevent the spread of sin and unknowingly thwart the gospel too. In fact, the heart of the Great Commission addresses people groups. Let's look at Jesus' commandment in Matthew 28:19: "Go, therefore, and make disciples of all nations, baptizing them in the name of the Father and of the Son and of the Holy Spirit."

The Greek word here for "nation" is *ethne*, which means "a people, a nation, or a class." In other words, it's a people group. And it's not one that is distinguished purely by ethnicity or geographic location. People groups refer to any cultural distinction, no matter how obvious or subtle. My hardworking relatives in rural Ohio require a different kind of church than I do. The community of intellectuals in Boston is less apt to enjoy my preferred worship environment here in the resort town of Virginia Beach. And if you're planning to start a church in southern Maryland, you'd better know something about the Catholic heritage that preceded you.

When God chose to manifest his Holy Spirit to the Jews from every nation under heaven (Acts 2), he related this truth to each culture in its own language. He didn't unify the language; he adapted the message.

My People Group Epiphany

Crowds come together in people groups. I'm not a sociologist, but from the little that I know about human nature, we like hanging out with people just like us. My wife and I are certified trainers of the Myers-Briggs Type Indicator, a personality assessment tool. We've assessed dozens of church staffs to help them work better together. From years of analysis, we discovered that church staffs are largely made up of people just like one another. In fact, when senior pastors have personnel problems, they tend to be just personality differences due to conflicting temperaments. They hire and fire based largely on mutual compatibility. That's not exactly God's intention, to be sure, but I agree it's a much easier coexistence.

While serving as a collegiate pastor at a large, traditional church in Virginia Beach, Virginia, I was frustrated by my inability to reach anyone not like us. As a flagship congregation, we had become the default church for anyone in our denomination who moved into the area. Between you and me, I didn't even have to do outreach. The local military base kept bringing new people into our church. I felt like an activities director on a large Christian cruise ship.

One night, while Ainsley and I were walking through Town Point Park in downtown Norfolk, we spotted a large concert near the harbor. It was one of those hip, after-work parties sponsored by a local rock station to attract young twentysomethings. And it worked. Thousands of young adults were sipping drinks and watching the show. Seeing this fueled even greater frustration with my church. I had tried like mad to host concerts, parties, and social events to attract unchurched young adults but just couldn't do it.

But seeing this outdoor concert yielded my greatest epiphany for church planting. And it forever changed how I thought about reaching people.

As I looked out over the crowd, I noticed that it wasn't just one big sea of people all facing the stage. Rather it was made up of hundreds of small groups of four to six people hanging out together. Altogether they made up a really large crowd, even though they came for different purposes and with different friends.

God reminded me of Acts 20:20, where Paul says, "I did not shrink back from proclaiming to you anything that was profitable, or from teaching it to you in public and from house to house." In other words, churches have always been planted and the gospel has always been spread through pockets of people. We like to romanticize the New Testament, but I'm pretty sure these early Christians met from house to house because they couldn't stand to be around certain other people. (I'm only kidding . . . partly.) But they did see the world through different lenses of culture, personality, background, and language. These small groups came together because of cultural affinity.

Contextualizing the Gospel

Contextualizing the gospel in each of our churches is exactly what God had in mind for the Great Commission and for church planting. If he wanted all of our churches to be the same, he would have called only like-minded church planters. Instead, he wired you with the right personality, gift mix, background, and experience to reach a specific group of people. And we'll do a great job of it as long as we don't try to be someone else in the process. How many pastors do you know who have admitted to wearing suits and preaching like their heroes of the faith in the early years? Plenty.

Let me be perfectly clear about this. You're not only allowed to plant a different kind of church for a specific group of people; you're commanded to do it. The Bible is filled with communities of faith that were formed around cultural distinctives. In Acts 6, some Greek Christian widows are complaining about low food rations. So to respond to the problem, the apostles appoint deacons, almost all of which happen to be Greek. Coincidence?

In Matthew 9:9–10 Jesus calls a tax collector named Matthew to leave his business and follow him. The first thing Matthew does is invite Jesus to a party for his tax collector buddies. As a colleague in the industry, Matthew is the only one who can reach these guys. They are never going to come to the seaside revivals Jesus was holding for fishermen. So what does Matthew do? He hosts a special gathering where his tax collector friends can feel at home. He contextualizes the gospel for them. Notice he doesn't compromise it, but he does contextualize it for them.

As we read through the New Testament, a Greek word keeps popping up to describe these subgroups, these culturally distinct people groups. It's *oikos*, and it means "household." Today when we think of our household, we think of immediate family members and maybe the dog. But the ancient concept of household included everyone in your family—your servants, your peers, and your community. Essentially, it was your people group. These were the people with whom you shared life.

Time and time again throughout the Scriptures, we see entire *oikos*, or households, coming to faith in Jesus. In Acts 16:14–15, Lydia's *oikos* in Philippi trusts in Jesus together. In Acts 16:29–34, a Roman jailer's *oikos* becomes converted.

And in Acts 18:8, Crispus, the synagogue ruler, comes to faith by way of *oikos*. These weren't robotic conversions, where the kids were dragged kicking and screaming into faith. These were community-wide acceptances of the gospel because it was contextualized specifically for their people group.

A Contextualized God

God is a contextualizing God, so we must be contextualizing ministers. In Philippians 2:5–8, Jesus did not consider his deity something to be grasped, to be held on to. But, rather, out of his great love for us, he made himself of no reputation, taking the form of a human, appearing in the likeness of man, a servant. This is the greatest act of contextualizing the gospel that has ever been done. Any of our efforts—just in case we're worried about taking it too far—will pale in comparison. Jesus effectively "incarnated" the gospel, and not only are we allowed to do this, but we are commanded to do it. We are to meet people where they are, not present the gospel or plant churches in a way that requires them to meet us. Repentance is hard enough without having to jump through hoops we create.

Much of what we think is the gospel is actually our own cultural preference. And typically, the more demanding our form of church, the farther away from the true gospel it is. After all, Jesus came to us. He became one of us.

Conversion requires repentance. And I don't advocate an easy gospel or any form of faith that's not founded on complete and utter dependence on God. But if we stop short of what Jesus did to meet us where we are by coming to earth as a human, we're far less biblical than we think we are.

Scandalously Biblical

My church planting friend, Vince Antonucci, has a remarkable testimony and a remarkable church. His mother was a Jew, and his father was a professional poker player who ended up in jail. Vince never stepped foot into a church until he was in college. You can read the entire story in his book *I Became a Christian and All I Got Was This Lousy T-Shirt*. Out of his radical salvation experience, Vince came away with an incredible passion for lost people. When Vince started his first church, he refused to let too many Christians join him. He didn't want the expectations of having any other purpose but reaching lost people.

I learned about Vince because he was planting Forefront Church in Virginia Beach while I was working at the traditional church. I heard his ads on secular radio stations. I saw the kinds of people who attended his church. And the one time I visited, I sat near people who smelled like beer and cigarette smoke. Vince was clearly reaching people far from God, and he was taking a lot of heat for it. Still, Vince's compassion for lost people has continued to grow.

Vince recently moved to Las Vegas where he started Verve, a church to reach people whose lives are shattered by the town's gambling and sex industry. He launched his church right on the Vegas strip where few churches have dared to go. Maybe it's Vince's compassion for his parents. Maybe it's because Vince was once radically unchurched as well. Or maybe it's because we're all commissioned by Jesus to meet people where they are. But Vince's desire to incarnate the gospel is scandalously biblical.

Cultures and Caste Systems

Donald McGavran was the first person to articulate the concept of reaching people groups. McGavran was a missionary to India in the mid-1900s and is known as the father of church growth. He tried unsuccessfully for years to plant churches that would unify the Indian people. They're divided into caste systems, social strata that limit or increase their opportunities for success. The entire fabric of the Indian people is based on these social divisions. In Donald's earliest attempts to reach everyone, the Brahmans refused to attend with the Vaishyas, and the Shudras refused to attend with the Kshatriyas, and so on.

When all of Donald's methods failed, he resorted to a tactic that would change the face of missions. That is, he started planting churches within caste systems. The result was a number of thriving, growing churches that attracted people within social castes. Donald came to understand that effective evangelism isn't only theological; it's also sociological.

Culture Clusters

No matter what you think of other churches and how they worship, you can't deny that God uses them too. And no matter how integrated we'd like churches to be, they will always be made up of clusters of like-minded people.

Many congregations are formed around an emphasis on certain spiritual gifts. Teaching, for example. I know churches that are led by great teachers, and other great teachers attend because of it. It's great teachers who are listening to other great teachers like one big teaching utopia. Seems like a waste to me when so many other churches need good teachers added to their focus on worship and serving. Yet God uses these churches to reach people who care about biblical accuracy and truth.

Some churches are shepherded by strong leaders. Their presence exudes leadership and charisma. Countless other leaders follow them because they attract people who want to be part of something great. It feels like a celebrity culture to me, but God uses these living legends to draw scores of people to himself.

I know of more and more churches that place earplug dispensers in their lobbies because the worship is so loud. For the people who attend these services, extremely loud music is their conduit for worshipping God. It seems like a turnoff to elderly people and those with more refined tastes in music, but these churches are uniquely positioned to reach a special class of worshipper.

Every Church Contextualizes

The truth is, every church plant contextualizes for a particular culture. It just might not be the culture around it. Or the same era. The pastor of Capitol Hill Baptist Church in Washington, DC, Mark Dever, once joked that his church had contextualized to the '90s . . . the 1690s. But Dr. Dever is onto something. He knows his community on Capitol Hill. He knows that highly educated government leaders respond better to a more historical approach to the gospel and to church. Dever's liturgical services and content-rich sermons appeal to a community with more PhDs per capita than anywhere else in the country.

Every church contextualizes. The only question is to which culture. To answer this question for yourself, look hard at your community and the people God has wired you to reach. When you find this cultural sweet spot, the movement that is your church plant will spread rapidly throughout this community.

In the final chapter of this section, we'll look at how to nurture this movement.

10

NURTURING A MOVEMENT

An Expanding Radius of Influence

Once your rock starts rolling, the goal is to keep it moving. Your church will either continue influencing the community and impacting people's lives, or it will stall out and become a living monument. And the minute your congregation decides to exist for itself, the church is dead. Sadly, new churches can hang around long past their funerals. Inwardly focused communities are shockingly resilient. I once observed a core group survive seven years past its founder's departure. The members were highly committed but never reached anyone else; they weren't interested in fresh vision. They spent most Sunday mornings simply enjoying breakfast together with spiritual overtones, and they liked it that way.

Paul made a groundbreaking statement to the church of Corinth that ought to forever change how we view our churches: "We have the hope that as your faith increases, our area of ministry will be greatly enlarged, so that we may preach the gospel to the regions beyond you" (2 Cor. 10:15–16).

This is brilliant. Paul is essentially saying, "When I was with you, I created a radius of impact in your community. And when I return, I'd like it to be larger."

Paul viewed the gospel movement through an apostolic lens. This was his calling. He saw geography, people groups, and circles of influence that he hoped would grow larger and larger. He wanted the gospel to spread like a holy virus throughout the world, and he had little tolerance for trying to reach the already reached. He was the Captain Jean Luc Picard of missions. He wanted to go where no one had gone before. For him, it was the work of pastors and elders to nurture the movement he catalyzed. He would, of course, come back and check on them.

Don't Screw Up

The gospel is a movement. Your church plant is a movement. And once it starts rolling, your job is to not screw it up. Reproduction, duplication, continuation—whatever you call it, Jesus banked on it when he gave us the Great Commission. He said to go "make disciples" not "converts" because the spread of the gospel depended on a higher level of commitment. You've got to marvel at the amount of trust Jesus put into his ragtag band of Hebrew school dropouts to spread the gospel. Yet they did it. Here you and I are, two thousand years later, still working to keep the movement going.

When you read through Paul's letters, you see that he spends much of his time providing tips for not screwing up the movement of the gospel. And he admits as much in 2 Corinthians 13:7–8: "Now we pray to God that you do nothing wrong, not that we may appear to pass the test, but that you may do what is right, even though we may appear to fail. For we are not able to do anything against the truth, but only for the truth."

"We pray that you won't do anything wrong." Paul knew how easy it was for obstructions to come in the way of the gospel movement. In 2 Corinthians 6:3, Paul writes, "We put no stumbling block in anyone's path, so that our ministry will not be discredited" (NIV). In 2 Corinthians 11:9 he writes, "And when I was with you and needed something, I was not a burden to anyone. . . . I have kept myself from being a burden to you in any way, and will continue to do so" (NIV).

Paul's concern was for the unimpeded movement of the gospel. He saw any barrier to the gospel as a stumbling block that must be removed.

Sweeping the Trail

Do you remember the story of the Oregon Trail from your fifth-grade history class? In the nineteenth century, pioneers traveled west from Missouri to Oregon to expand the settlement of America from the Atlantic to the Pacific Ocean. I remember learning that the only way they could traverse the wild terrain in their covered wagons was to send people ahead to remove rocks and debris from the trail. These trail sweepers went ahead of the wagon train to make sure the path was unimpeded. I suspect this was the hardest job in pioneering. But their sacrificial efforts made the journey much less difficult and changed the way of life for a new nation of people.

Physical rocks and debris don't thwart the movement of the gospel. But substantial barriers have to be removed if we want our churches to grow and to impact people. As ministers, our job is to be trail sweepers. It requires tremendous work, but removing obstacles makes the journey to Christ much less difficult and changes the way of life for a new nation of redeemed people.

Here are five barriers that must be removed for the gospel, and consequently our churches, to spread:

1. Financial Barriers

Every church plant has a financial burden that must be displaced for people to meet Jesus. Planting a church costs a lot of money. If we expect the people we're trying to reach to fund our efforts, we'll sabotage the gospel. After all, Jesus meant for salvation to be a free gift. If we try to turn our mission field into a venture capital group, they'll reject both Jesus and us.

Paul understood this, which is why he removed the financial burden from his new churches. He either solicited donations from mature congregations, such as the church at Macedonia, or he worked a second job to keep the money coming in. For the first three years at Reston Community Church, we raised $80,000 each year from outside sources to avoid putting financial strain on our new congregation. We sent newsletters to friends, hosted fund-raising events at partner churches, and provided a monthly giving program to keep the money coming in. One year we even issued a Christmas catalog full of church supplies to acquire some much-needed items.

Paul also worked as a tent maker with Priscilla and Aquila during his ministry to displace the financial burden. In other words, Paul was bivocational. I remember thinking that I would never be bivocational. In some ways I felt like it was surrendering my hope for a great church. I didn't think I could work two jobs. And I certainly didn't want to get stuck doing something other than my calling. And besides, what was I going to do? Work at Home Depot? I'll be honest; you don't want me giving you home repair advice.

Let me say something briefly about the fear of bivocationalism.

Many church planters believe that leading a church is all they can do. They think their other vocational options are flipping burgers or schlepping Starbucks. So they quickly launch services to generate tithes. They hang on by their fingernails for years on end, waiting for the church to gain some financial momentum. They miss out on outreach opportunities right in front of them because the church has no money. And frustration begins to settle in with the people they're trying to reach.

But now that I've crossed over, I can't think of anything more liberating, more empowering, or more bridge-building than making tents. What's more, there's no better executive training program than church planting. Church planters are better qualified for top jobs than they think they are.

My church-planting friend Paul Gilmore got a high-level sales job at a tech company in Centreville, Virginia, by claiming in an interview that if he could get people in church on Sunday mornings, he could sell server space to clients. Today Paul could buy a Porsche and a mansion on his salary, but he funds his church plant instead. Even my own father, who was a pastor for years, has become one of the top training executives for the Association of Builders and Contractors. If you're planting a church, you've got the combination of an MBA and a ThD simply from life experience. There's no reason to be intimidated.

2. Leadership Barriers

One of the obvious barriers to church growth is leadership. When we fail to reproduce ourselves, the movement fizzles out. Some time ago I attended a Christian outreach event that was bursting at the seams. The leader confided that he was struggling to teach every week and minister to so many people. When I suggested that he reproduce himself, his answer surprised me. He said that none of the attendees would enjoy listening to anyone else, that no one taught the way he did. And frankly, I knew what he meant. He was a good teacher, and he had a fantastic way with people. In fact, he once tried to use someone else, but the group hated it. And he certainly didn't want to destroy the group.

Great leaders know how to empower others for long-term success. They find ways to sabotage the group's dependency on themselves and spread the leadership responsibilities. The more leaders you can equip and empower, the longer the movement can last. I later found out that this outreach didn't survive, and I can't help but think that the movement was built on an infrastructure that was too small. Namely him.

You've probably heard of both John Wesley and George Whitefield. They were ministry contemporaries in the 1700s. Both of them started in England and eventually made their way to America. Whitefield was known for his incredible stage presence and charisma; John Wesley, not so much. Both of these patriarchs were astonishing figures in the history of evangelical Christianity. But only one of them developed other leaders. John Wesley organized many of his new believers into small groups that grew deeper in faith through rigorous spiritual disciplines and relational accountability. The impact of John Wesley's disciple making is noticeable today. Whitefield's influence, on the other hand, disappeared with him. At the end of his ministry, Whitefield confessed: "My brother Wesley acted wisely—the souls that were awakened under his ministry, he joined in class, and thus preserved the fruits of his labor. This I neglected, and my people are a rope of sand."[1]

The apostle Paul understood the importance of reproducing leaders to the gospel's movement. He wrote in 2 Timothy 2:2: "And what you have heard from me in the presence of many witnesses, commit to faithful men who will be able to teach others also."

Without developing leaders, the movement of a church dies. It's ironic that what we *think* will kill momentum (i.e., taking a chance on someone else) is ultimately what preserves it. Great leaders know it doesn't solely depend on them.

Several weeks ago in southern California, I was amazed to find out that one of the fastest-growing church plants in the country, Rock Harbor Church, is led by someone who doesn't even preach most Sundays. Todd Proctor leads the pastoral staff, while teaching pastor Mike Erre addresses the congregation almost every week. What a rare demonstration of humility from both of them. And the church is much stronger for it.

3. Ethical Barriers

Every moral failure by a pastor puts a chink in the armor of Christianity. If you were to take a survey of people who oppose the Christian faith, I am certain that most people would say their objections are based on cases of Christian hypocrisy. And I don't blame them. When I was a child, our church's children's pastor ran off with another woman, leaving his wife to deal with their terminally ill child. A young Christian woman I know has been sexually propositioned by no less than four married, Christian men throughout her lifetime. If it weren't for the knowledge that even Christians are fallible, these incidents would have done far worse damage to our faith. When it happens to an unbeliever, on the other hand, the response is not quite so forgiving.

As church planters, the movement of the gospel is largely based on how we conduct ourselves. This is not a legalism thing. God forgives our mistakes, and we can be restored. But our mistakes can leave a negative impact on the lives of other people. God's grace does not necessarily restore goodwill. So it's imperative that we carry the gospel with a great sense of care and accountability. If you're a married church leader, don't get in the car alone with any other woman than your spouse. Don't stay alone in hotel rooms that have expanded cable channels. Confess your deepest, darkest secrets to a few trusted friends. Get a Christian counselor. And never let the work of ministry take preeminence over your family.

One of the best examples of spiritual accountability was Billy Graham's refusal to get into an elevator with a woman. This might seem a bit extreme, but Billy understood he importance of living above reproach as a messenger of the gospel. One time a newspaper reported a scandalous rumor that Billy had spent the night with a woman named Beverly Shea. The actual person in Graham's room that night, of course, was his favorite song leader George Beverly Shea.

These ethical roadblocks in ministry aren't just sexual in nature. More than other organizations, church plants can struggle with financial integrity. I'm not saying these are intentional abuses, but when the church planter is writing checks, depositing tithes, and handling the bookkeeping too, he's setting himself up for a fall. Even if he's not misusing funds, he's still vulnerable to accusations. One negative word can plant a seed of doubt in the congregation, and the planter's credibility is tossed out the window.

Another ethical roadblock to the gospel is the way people treat one another in the church. Congregational infight-
ing, gossip, and disunity can undermine the gospel faster than
anything else. In church plants, where change is frequent and
decisions are more democratic, it's easy to let division get
out of hand. I love what Jim Cymbala of the Brooklyn
Tabernacle asks all new members to acknowledge when they
join the church:

> One Sunday about twenty years ago, back in our days
> in the YMCA, I said something impromptu while
> receiving new members into the church that has stuck
> with us ever since. People were standing in a row
> across the front before me, and as I spoke, the Holy
> Spirit seemed to prompt me to add, "And now,
> I charge you, as pastor of this church, that if you ever
> hear another member speak an unkind word of
> criticism or slander against anyone—myself, another
> pastor, an usher, a choir member, or anyone else—you
> have the authority to stop that person in mid-
> sentence and say, 'Excuse me—who hurt you? Who
> ignored you? Who slighted you? Was it Pastor
> Cymbala? Let's go to his office right now. He will get
> on his knees and apologize to you, and then we'll pray
> together, so God can restore peace to this body. But
> we will not let you talk critically about people who
> are not present to defend themselves.' New members
> please understand that I am entirely serious about
> this. I want you to help resolve this kind of thing
> immediately. And meanwhile, know this: If you are
> ever the one doing the loose talking, we will confront
> you." To this very day, every time we receive new
> members, I say much the same thing. It is always a
> solemn moment. That is because I know what most
> easily destroys churches. It is not crack cocaine. It is

not government oppression. It is not lack of funds.
Rather, it is gossip and slander that grieves the Holy
Spirit.[2]

For the sake of countless people who don't yet know
Christ, seeds of contention must be uprooted quickly. And
there's no other way to do this than by following the principle of humble confrontation in Matthew 18:15–17. When
relationships are mutually submissive and people are uni-
fied, the path is cleared for the gospel movement to spread
more quickly.

4. Sociological Barriers

If I had hoped to make any point in this section, it was that
the gospel movement is not just theological or spiritual. It's
also sociological. Whether we like it or not, social forces
impact our church's success. Whenever guests walk into a
poorly attended church service, they can't help but think
something's wrong. It's not personal. It's just the way people
think. When Steven Furtick and Chunks Corbett started
Elevation Church in Charlotte, North Carolina, they cur-
tained off any unused portions of the room so that no matter
how many people attended, it always felt packed. They
worked to overcome these mental barriers.

As a church planter, there are some dues you simply
don't have to pay. Who told us we had to start off with the
odds stacked against us? When Stuart Hodges started Water's
Edge Church in Yorktown, Virginia, he resolved to launch a
church that appeared to be five years old. This meant he had
to raise more money, gather a larger core group, and start
with more developed ministries. Six years later Waters Edge
is reaching sixteen hundred people each week.

Sometimes change can present psychological barriers.
People don't hate change, just the change they don't like,

which is most of it. When our church first launched in Reston, we had to move to a new meeting location about once a year. And every time we moved, we lost at least 25 percent of our congregation. People had great excuses: the new location was too far away; they'd been meaning to leave anyway; they weren't sure they'd embraced the vision. But at the root of it, people simply didn't like the kind of changes we were making. In most of these cases, I couldn't stop the changes. We were forced to move because of one circumstance or another. I learned that people aren't as entrepreneurial as their church planting leaders. And if we constantly create chaos, it unsettles people right out the door.

5. Relevancy Barriers

Every night while driving home from work, I drive by a church that has one of those infamous church signs. Every week it features a new message that gives me a different reason not to attend. Who cares what your Sunday night sermon title is? Why would I ever come to your Saturday morning men's breakfast uninvited? I'm sure I'm not the only one who is baffled by these messages. But it's not just church signs that put off people; it's a whole smorgasbord of reasons. It's the spiritual language we use, the culture we create in the church, the tone of our sermons, and the kind of music we play. Many outsiders feel like they stepped into a world with its own culture and customs. Many church plants are simply not relevant.

I'm not saying we should try to keep up with the preferences of outsiders to the detriment of our Christian community. Nor am I saying that we should paint the gospel in gentler hues. But much of what we do is rooted in our Christian biases and preferences. Brian Bloye, who once served at Jerry Falwell's Thomas Road Baptist Church and then started a successful church in Dallas, Georgia, said it took several years to adjust his Lynchburg way of thinking.

I'm not recommending that we compromise the gospel message or downplay the spiritual content of our services. I'm recommending that we detox from a previous way of doing church. If we want to remove barriers to the gospel, we have to immerse ourselves in the local culture and learn to speak its language. We have to build bridges to our community so that people can easily cross.

Building In-Roads

Jesus didn't present the gospel without preparing the way for it. His cousin John's lifelong purpose was to act as a trail sweeper for the Messiah. Jesus didn't see the gospel as merely a belief system but as a movement, and he provided for its continuance. Before Jesus stepped foot in Samaria and Judea, his disciples had gone ahead of him. And before he introduced the gospel to the Jews, he had given them training wheels through the old covenant to prepare them for it.

One of the greatest historical examples of removing barriers to the gospel was Alexander the Great's empirical rule three hundred years before Christ. Does that surprise you? Before Alexander's time the ancient world was divided by geographic terrain and significant language differences. But as the Greco-Roman Empire spread throughout the Mediterranean world, Alexander united it with advanced roadways and one common language—Koiné Greek. God chose to reveal the gospel at this distinct moment in history so that it would spread easily throughout the world.

Church as a Movement

As messengers of the gospel, we start new churches in order to congregate believers and build spiritual communities that reflect the glory of God. The reason we work so hard to remove barriers and keep the movement going is because this is how Christ is manifest throughout the world. The more God-glorifying churches we can plant, the more people can experience his grace, forgiveness, restoration, and love. This is a movement worth spreading.

There are people in your church who are better at spreading it than others. They are naturals at connecting people. It's not necessarily a spiritual thing; they're just good at building relationships. To make the most of your movement as a church plant, you have to identify these people.

Several years ago I diagrammed the names of every committed person in our church on a piece of paper. As the founding pastor, I started with myself in the middle and then worked outward, adding people I had invited who then invited other people. When I finished this exercise, the resulting diagram was incredibly insightful. I noticed there were a few people who had invited more people than others. Some had invited no one. Oftentimes one invitation spawned large numbers of other guests. Again, this is not a spiritual issue. Some people simply know how to leverage relationships better than others.

When I saw the results, I decided to encourage and support these connectors. I gave them Starbucks gift cards to take friends out for coffee. I asked for their opinions on outreach events and special services. Essentially, I started investing in our highest-yield accounts. Not everyone in your church can help you further the movement. Nor should they be made to feel guilty if they don't. But fueling a movement is about identifying your connectors and enabling them to reach even more people. This is what Jesus did by investing in twelve disciples to keep the movement going from his time until ours. Our job is to keep paying it forward. People have bled, sweated, and died to ensure that you and I would hear this life-saving message.

The question is, what will you do with it?

Notes

1. Stephen Tomkins, *John Wesley: A Biography* (Wm. B. Eerdmans Publishing Company, 2003), 128.
2. Jim Cymbala, *Fresh Wind, Fresh Fire* (Grand Rapids, MI: Zondervan, 2003), 160.

QUESTIONS FROM PART 2

No Mo

1. What odds are stacked against you as a church planter?
2. How is idealism helping you as a church planter?
3. How could idealism hurt you as a church planter?
4. Where do you see momentum working for you?
5. With what wounds are you ministering right now?

Challenge: Find two to three friends in ministry who will be honest with you and allow you to be honest with them. Hard times are ahead, and you'll need these partners in ministry to get you through them.

Momentum-Based Church Planting

1. What social network has God been building around you to become his church?
2. Have you ever spotted a church in the making, yours or someone else's?
3. Have you spent enough time caring for the people you hope to reach?

4. If you think of your church plant as a rock, is it rolling or sitting still?
5. What principles of momentum have you disregarded in starting a church?

Challenge: Identify where God is moving around you, and figure out how to join that movement. Maybe it's joining a network of churches, inviting another leader to coffee, or serving in-residence at another local church. But look for momentum.

The Anatomy of a Crowd

1. What outreaches aren't working for you? Why do you think that might be?
2. What are some ways to make multitudes before presenting the gospel?
3. What natural gifts has God given you to make multitudes?
4. How might your preferences be getting in the way of reaching people?
5. How can you meet people where they are?

Challenge: Pretend you're not a church planter for a moment. What business would you start in your community? What charitable organization would you start? In other words, how would you connect with people apart from the gospel?

People Groups

1. What kinds of people make up the community around you?
2. Which of these people are you best suited to reach?

3. What form of church will you need to create for these people?
4. You can't reach everybody. What kinds of people will you probably not reach?
5. How might your spiritual gifts impact the kinds of people you reach?

Challenge: Create a profile for the kinds of people you are most likely to reach. List their age range, geographic location, stage of life, lifestyle preferences, socioeconomic status, whatever comes to mind.

Nurturing a Movement

1. What barriers are keeping people from accepting Jesus in your community?
2. Would you be willing to be bivocational if it helped spread the gospel?
3. How are you empowering other leaders in your church?
4. What changes have you made that caused people to leave your church?
5. In what ways do you need to detox from your previous way of doing church?

Challenge: Create a diagram that shows how people came into your church. Who invited whom? Now identify your most effective connectors and pour into them.

Part 3

DEEP ROOTS

11

FOREIGN FIELDS

Shallow Roots

One afternoon I went to a scheduled lunch meeting with two members from my church's leadership team. We were getting ready to move our church into a local elementary school because the cockroaches were getting bad in the movie theater, and parents were starting to complain. Not only that, but this particular theater was tucked in the back of a shopping center where no one could see us from the road. We needed to get out of there.

For me it was an exciting time. We had been waiting over a year for a school to open, and this was finally our big break. We dreamed of reaching more families, interacting with people in the neighborhood, and having more space for our children's ministry. The two leaders I came to meet had been my champions, my prayer warriors. They had even helped me find the location. But when I showed up at the restaurant, one of them had arrived early and asked to speak with me before the other arrived.

"Can we talk?" he asked.

"Of course," I said, sensing a bit of awkwardness.

"I won't be making the move with the church," he said.

He offered a few reasons for moving on, none of which felt justifiable to me. But I could tell he was pained by this decision. I was blindsided by the news. He had been one of my closest friends in the church. He had shared my vision for ministry. We dreamed and prayed together for the church's future. He'd helped me start the church, for crying out loud. I was shell-shocked by his decision. But it wasn't the last time I experienced one of these conversations.

Over the next five years I saw friend after friend walk away from the church. Some of them had philosophical differences with me. Others wanted "deeper teaching" or age-specific programs for their children. For some, all it took was a change of location to send them packing. And each and every time, I felt like my heart was being ripped out of my chest.

At first I found myself getting angry. I would compile mental lists of why they were wrong, spiritually immature, or consumeristic. I'd lobby endlessly for them to overlook their differences and stay involved. But eventually I realized that no matter what I said or did, I could never change their minds. By the time they were telling me, it was already too late. We always parted amicably. I only remember a few incidents when people left upset. I tried to be peaceful and gracious as people moved on.

To this day I can remember every "breakup conversation" I had as a church planter. They were grueling. All of them.

I'd love to tell you that I became more spiritually mature in my responses over time, but honestly, I think I just became numb. Whenever a couple would call and ask to meet with

me to talk about the church, I knew what it meant. To protect myself, I'd outright ask them if they were leaving. They
would stammer for a few minutes about how the church
just wasn't meeting their needs, and then I'd say, "Listen,
there's no sense in our getting together to talk about something you've already decided. I completely understand, and
you will greatly be missed." This always caught them off
guard, but I had been through too many heart-wrenching
conversations to believe it would help if we got together.
Granted, it might have helped them get closure, but I just
couldn't take it anymore.

Redefining Commitment

After losing a heartbreaking number of people whom
I thought were committed, I asked myself a soul-searching
question: How in the world could Ainsley and I be the only
ones who are invested in our church plant? How could some
of our closest friends sweat, bleed, and cry with us through
the trials of church planting and then walk away? Didn't
these people want a new church? Hadn't God brought them
to partner with us? Isn't that why they came? They had
already invested so much. We had shared celebrations and
sins with one another, dreamed, and cried together. How
could we have not seen this coming?

I once read where Steve Sjogren, founder of the
Cincinnati Vineyard Church, said that a core group is like
scaffolding. God brings them in temporarily to help build
the walls of the church. But once the walls are in place, God
takes them away. This soothed me for a few years. It helped
me accept the departure of good friends in hopes of drawing
even better ones. But then I started seeing other successful
church plants retain their people, and the attrition rate at my

church never stopped. Between you and me, I'm still licking my wounds today.

The Truth about Commitment

The truth is, these friends were committed to the church . . . just not like I was. The dream wasn't birthed out of their hearts. They were simply helping us because they liked us. Their commitment to us was tied to something other than the vision. And when my relationship with them changed as the church grew, the vision wasn't enough to hold them. All of this time I had assumed they felt everything I felt, believed everything I believed, saw the community through my eyes. But I had a shallow history with them. I had only known them for several years at most. The church was not birthed out of us as a community. They were simply responding to my vision, my salesmanship.

Hindsight being twenty-twenty, I should have seen it coming. A common characteristic defined all of those who left: they were all Christians who had come from other churches. And some of them couldn't be pulled entirely from the churches of their past—their long, memory-rich past. Their faith stories hadn't originated in our church but in other ministries and spiritual relationships. They didn't owe our church their lives; it was simply a good cause, a weekend charity at best.

How did this come about? Easy. Ainsley and I weren't from the area. We had no long-term history with these people. We were strangers from a faraway land, missionaries in a foreign field. We felt loved, to be sure. But after just a few short years, the vision could only take them so far. They had no personal experience with the mission we upheld. They were sold on a theoretical mission, not one they had personally experienced. After seven years of planting a church, it became clear that our most committed colaborers were the people who had found Jesus through our ministry. After all, they knew it worked! They believed in the mission because they were impacted by it. They owed us their lives.

The Deeply Committed

In a church plant, your most committed people will be those whose lives have been impacted by the ministry of your church. No one else will believe as strongly in your vision as someone who owes her life to it. When you launch a church that is sprung out of long-term friendships and existing community, the loyalty is built in. The vision isn't foreign; it's already been gaining momentum in the community.

But for those who start from scratch, it takes years of building a committed core. In this case your role is not that of a church planter. It's that of a missionary: someone who first exposes people to Jesus, shares life with them, and then gives them a reason to form community. And when I say, "Be a missionary," I mean someone who builds relationships first and creates trust so that the barriers to the gospel can be removed and a successful church can be planted.

Community Compatibility

I've always been intrigued by organ transplants, the idea that your body decides whether it will accept the new replacement or not. When Ainsley and I transplanted ourselves from Virginia Beach to the suburbs of Washington, DC, to plant a church in 2001, I felt the same way. I kept wondering if the community would accept us or reject us. It took about four years for the transplant to take, and those definitely weren't easy years.

Every community has its own network of influencers, power brokers, and thought leaders who either bless or curse the newcomers. They don't do this officially, of course. But their words and actions carry tremendous influence. You'd think this "townspeople effect" would have died years ago with Harriet Olson and *Little House on the Prairie*, but it's alive and well in your community too. Outsiders are always held under suspicion. What people don't know, they don't trust. And for many transplanted church planters, it takes years for them to be accepted by the local community.

Homegrown Church Planters

Time and again I notice that most church planters who succeed are indigenous to their communities. My friend Larry Rising planted a successful church in the Shenandoah Mountain region of Virginia, and he unapologetically admits, "These are my people." They have strong, southern accents, an incredible gift of hospitality, and a noticeable distrust of outsiders. If I tried to plant a church in rural Harrisonburg, Virginia, I'm pretty sure I'd fail. I don't talk like them, think like them, or act like them. To think that I could waltz in and succeed purely because of mission and passion is lunacy.

Stuart Hodges, who planted Water's Edge Church in Yorktown, Virginia, said he couldn't overemphasize the importance of planting a church in a community where you have roots. Deep roots. Stuart and his wife both attended high school and college in the same community where they planted a church. He said, "The longer you've been in a community, the smaller it becomes. It feels like we know everybody." Stuart shaved years off the start-up phase of his new church by being indigenous to the community.

A Considerate Rejection

Several years ago I got a call from a church planting friend who wanted to move from Tennessee to Washington, DC, to start a church. He told me that he had e-mailed a prominent pastor inside the beltway to ask for his advice. Apparently the pastor told him not to come, that as an outsider he probably wouldn't make it. When my friend heard this, he immediately thought the pastor was a controlling, selfish dictator who wanted the city for himself. This young planter called because he wanted to know what I thought.

"I think he's saving your life," I said.

Having observed DC's culture for five years by this time, I'd come to see that our nation's capital has a stronger than usual bias against new churches. If you're unfamiliar to them, you don't exist. The successful plants are started by insiders who take on DC's affection for academic and serious study. Almost all of the megachurch pastors in DC still wear suits, if that tells you anything. The only exceptions are churches that capture DC's cyclical intern population, running what are essentially young adult ministries for out-of-state transplants.

Planting Deeper Roots

When God creates a church in the making, he doesn't just call one person to start it. He calls a whole network of people who have been growing pregnant with vision. They may not be able to articulate it, but they have all experienced the fruit of living it. In other words, a church plant should not be just one person's idea. It's a vision born out of relationships, what God has been doing in the community all along.

If you're coming into a new community without this history, you're not a church planter; you're a missionary. Your job is to gather indigenous people and help them impact their own community in the language and culture with which they are familiar. You have to find the homegrown vision. I'm convinced that unless God calls us to be missionaries in new territories, our job is to look for the church he has been preparing around us. If we did this, we probably wouldn't have such a difficult time. The failure rate of new churches would drop dramatically.

Missed Opportunities

It's hard for me to admit this, but before Ainsley and I moved to northern Virginia, we had the chance to plant an indigenous church. Our vision for church planting came alive while I was working on staff at a large church in Virginia Beach. We saw scores of unreached young adults in our community and had a great desire to reach them. But our hands were tied by the traditional church where I was employed. We were dissuaded from reaching people outside of the established system of our church.

So Ainsley and I began experimenting on the side. We invited a few college-age students from outside the church to our apartment on Monday nights. We didn't lead a Bible study. We simply hung out. We talked, played games, laughed, and ate food that Ainsley prepared. Eventually the conversation came around to spiritual matters, and we talked in depth about the redeeming work of Jesus in every aspect of life. It was remarkable. It was even more remarkable that they came back week after week. They invited friends. They came early and stayed late. They didn't miss it. And people's lives were starting to change. What we had was a church in the making.

When I approached my senior pastor about the idea of planting another local church, he wouldn't hear of it. In fact, he called our denominational leaders and asked them to send me as far away from Virginia Beach as possible. His church was in the middle of a significant building campaign, and I suspect he didn't want to lose people or money. He couldn't understand the need for another church.

When we announced to the church that we were resigning and moving to plant a church, the feedback was surprising. An entire group of people asked us to stay and plant a church with them. They loved us and had grown highly committed to our vision. In fact, one wealthy family offered to support us financially if we stayed. Another lady offered to sell us her home at an extreme discount. At the time we were encouraged by their love and support, but we were too idealistic to change our minds. Looking back at that experience now, I realize we missed out on a church in the making.

God had been building and shaping a spiritual community all around us, and we never even realized it. Now that I'm years removed from the experience, I wonder if prayer and persistent nudging might have changed my pastor's heart. I wonder if we gave up too easily. But all of that is neither here nor there. We're in awe of how God used us as missionaries in northern Virginia.

Still it doesn't stop me from encouraging other planters to look around at their circumstances. Where is God moving? Who is becoming committed to you and your vision? Is it a vision with which your community is pregnant, or are you inflicting a vision upon them instead?

Unequipped to Go It Alone

Think about it. Why would God give church planters only two or three prominent spiritual gifts if they were meant to start alone? There's a lot of talk about how we are "gifted" in ministry, but I believe it's much more accurate to say that we are "handicapped." The body of Christ is complete in its manifestation only through the local church. God has endowed believers in such a way that when they come together, all of our parts become knit together into a beautiful, albeit fallen, assembly of gifts. So when a church planter tries to go it alone or start from scratch, he is seriously handicapped. With only two or three prominent spiritual gifts, he will be limping along at best.

The most effective church plants launch with a team. They're made up of a community of people who are highly committed to the vision because they know one another, they're committed to the leader, and they understand the culture. Do you know the feeling of planting a church with a group of partners in ministry? People who are highly committed and truly share the vision? It's a completely different experience.

But the reality is that most church planters get stuck trying to convince random strangers to join their new church and end up doing it alone. They prepare the sermons and do the outreach and create the bulletins and design the Web site and run the youth ministry. And anything they feel unsuited to do is handed off to their wives. Talk about a miserable existence.

Despite our tendency as pastors to make things harder than they need to be, it's OK to plant a church with a team. After all, it was God's idea. He sent his disciples out in pairs. He prayed for the disciples' unity. He appointed partners in ministry for the apostle Paul. Church planting doesn't have to be an isolating, solitary endeavor. It can be a band of brothers, a sorority of sisters, and a fraternity of friends on mission.

The big question is how to do it. How do you create a church that can survive attrition? How do you plant deep roots? How do you launch a church out of the community?

We go there now.

12

INDIGENOUS PLANTS

Not Native

Growing up in Ohio, one of my favorite places to visit was a small, overlooked town called Sinking Spring, just north of the Kentucky border. It was home to some of my relatives on my mother's side of the family. We visited their farms, rode on their tractors, and listened to their stories on my grandmother's front porch. But my favorite reason for visiting was to explore the Native American history of southern Ohio. It's still populated with undisturbed burial mounds and mountaintop forts left over from the American Indians who once lived there. The town is far enough off the beaten path that you can still find ancient artifacts if you look carefully in the creek beds and cornfields.

One of the most notable burial mounds is Serpent Mound, a 1,330-foot-long mound of dirt formed into the shape of a snake swallowing an egg. The park service has provided an elevated viewing platform so that guests can see it from a bird's-eye view. When you consider that the serpent's curves line up with a particular constellation in the night sky, it really is a remarkable sight to behold. What's even more impressive is that geologists have tested the dirt that was used to build the mound and discovered that it's not native to any part of Ohio. In other words, the dirt is not indigenous. It is foreign, imported soil. To this day, geologists don't know where it came from. The Native Americans must have hauled it from some distance.

Fascinating, right?

The Church Planting Mystery

Mysterious transplants are a fascinating study. The trouble is, we carry this same fascination over to the idea of transplanted church planters. We hear stories about ambitious, young visionaries who prayed over a map until God revealed their target city like an epiphany from Gabriel. We hear about them packing up their cars without a plan and moving to strange cities to take them by storm. We all know these stories, and they embolden us. They give us hope that all we need is enough faith and determination, and we too can succeed. And to be sure, these stories do happen from time to time. A church planter may, in fact, accidentally land on the perfect context for his vision. But it's not the most likely scenario.

The Indigenous Church Plant

Most successful church plants are not the product of imported visions. They were the deliberate effort of a local leader to meet a need in his own community. They were started by leaders who had a deep understanding of their own towns. They were started by friends who had a rich history and a strong commitment to one another. They were started by people who understood what kind of church was needed in a particular community. Even if they couldn't articulate it, these indigenous planters sensed what would work best.

A transplanted church planter can't do this. He can't read between the lines. He can't know the community's culture. He doesn't have the deep relationships that successful plants require. And he doesn't know what kinds of churches are already thriving. He's never considered the ecclesiographics.

The most effective church plants were not imported; they were homegrown. They were not introduced to a community; they were invited. The story of how a church got started is too often dismissed when, in fact, it had everything to do with its success. We miss this however. We overlook how churches got started. We look at their success today when we should be looking at their pasts.

They Were Invited

When Jerry Falwell graduated from Baptist Bible College at the age of twenty-two, he was invited by thirty-five people to start Thomas Road Baptist Church. He didn't endeavor to do this on his own; he was invited. These thirty-five core group members from Park Avenue Baptist Church in Lynchburg were going to start the church with or without him. In fact, Jerry was on his way to Macon, Georgia, to start a different church before changing his mind. He joined a church in the making. I don't say all this to diminish this faith story. In fact, Jerry Falwell was one of the greatest men of faith I've ever seen. But this story needs to be told to demonstrate how God initiates a church long before we start it.

When Mark Batterson moved to Washington, DC, in the early 1990s, it wasn't to start a church. He had taken a job to create a satellite Bible college for laypeople in the district. But a group of nineteen people asked him to lead their new congregation, and National Community Church was born. Mark was joining a church in the making.

When my friend Daniel Floyd launched Lifepoint Church in Fredericksburg, Virginia, he was invited to do so by fifty core group members from another local church plant whose pastor had abandoned them. Lifepoint has exploded in growth because it was a church in the making.

My friend Mike Minter started Reston Bible Church in Virginia because a core group invited him to move from Florida. There were about one hundred people in Grapevine, Texas, who invited Ed Young Jr. to start Fellowship Church with them. Erwin McManus turned the existing Church at Brady in Los Angeles into Mosaic. Matt Chandler created The Village Church out of the remnant of First Baptist Church of Highland Village. The list goes on and on. Churches in the making practically beckon the planter to lead them!

When God creates a church in the making, he invites you to be a part of it. Our job is not to try to initiate the work of God but to respond to it.

Every Church Fulfills a Purpose

I've been told that we can't have enough church plants in one city, that there are far too few churches to reach everyone in a community. But this is dangerous advice. It assumes that everyone in town is immediately ready to start attending a church at any given time. But unfortunately they're not. The truth is, it is indeed possible to have too many churches if they're all the same kind of churches. In this case there will be winners, and there will be losers.

Every church fulfills a distinct purpose in a local community. And there's not much tolerance for overlap. If your approach to doing church is the same as another church's approach, one church will clearly win out, and it's usually the one that can do it better.

Like it or not, churches tend to colonize people by spiritual affinity. Each one feels its approach is the most biblical. But they're actually just congregating people who have a similar spiritual worldview. Below I've listed several niches that a church can occupy in a local community. This is not an exhaustive list; I'm generalizing a bit. But it will give you some idea of how churches colonize.

The Teaching Church

A strong teacher will attract people with the spiritual gift of teaching. This is the way they feel most engaged in a worship service—through study and an academic approach to faith. People who attend teaching churches show up with a Bible and a notebook in hand. They tell others about what good teaching they get on Sunday morning and how other churches don't feed them like this one does. Their view of the church is based on the content it provides. They're looking to be spiritually educated, and other approaches just aren't as enriching to them.

The Relational Church

Churches that emphasize community tend to gather highly relational people. Spiritual expression for them is about small groups, get-togethers, churchwide dinners and fellowship. This kind of church believes that loving people is the most important aspect of the Christian faith. They often attract broken people in need of grace. They believe that people are converted to community before they're converted to Christ. These kinds of churches engage in deep community with one another and attract people who feel the same way.

The Missions Church

Missions churches are driven toward overseas outreach. They set aside large portions of their budget to fund missionaries and send groups on mission trips. They hang large maps of the world on the wall and list the "missionaries of the month" in the prayer calendar. To these churches it's all about reaching the nations, and the local community becomes less of a concern than the global plight of the gospel.

The Outreach Church

The outreach church unashamedly designs their services for unchurched people. They're highly oriented toward reaching the lost and making sure their environment will embrace outsiders. The music is edgy; the sermons are based on pop culture; and the marketing is aggressive. To these churches deeper teaching is not only irrelevant but also prohibitive to a newcomer. After all, that's what discipleship classes are for. What's important now is making sure people find a saving relationship with Jesus. They see the church as a rescue station rather than a classroom.

The Megachurch

The megachurch is popular because it can afford to do things with excellence and offer programs for every age. It becomes the default church for the community because there's little risk or obligation for attendees. You can come and go as you please without hurting feelings or making a big deal about it.

The megachurch allows people to remain anonymous until they decide to get involved. The church may feel like a mall, but the music suits everyone, and the pastor consistently delivers an excellent message. Plus, it makes an easy choice for the community to attend. People are drawn to winning organizations. They don't have time to research the perfect church among the hundreds of options.

The Mercy Church

Churches that emphasize the grace of God tend to attract people who crave the assurance of it. The pastor often has a personal history that spurs this passion. These churches offer twelve-step programs, weeknight meetings for recovering addicts, and sermons that address recovery issues. Mercy churches partner with local homeless shelters and social justice causes. They want Christianity to be known for the humanitarian side of Christ. They care deeply about marginalized members of society.

The Denominational Church

Denominations are highly regarded by the traditionalists in our communities, and these churches scratch right where they itch. The flagship churches in a community use the denomination's mantras, raise money for denominational projects, and view their success in light of the denomination's benchmarks. They're proud to be affiliated with an umbrella organization and align their expression of faith to this particular label. To these traditionalists church planting is less important than the success of the flagship church.

The High Church

The high church is heavy on liturgy and tends to attract people who see their faith expressed through structure. The tone is solemn and the content is familiar—maybe not understandable but familiar. The attendees take great satisfaction in reciting passages and carrying out the sacraments. They prefer their services long and their preachers robed. Church is more of a ritual to be performed than a community to be shared or a mission to be pursued.

Identifying Your Niche

If a church plant tries to occupy the same space as an established church, it will always struggle to catch up. In church-going communities there are clear winners and clear losers. And usually the first church to occupy one space, or do it better, becomes the winner. The trouble with most struggling church plants is that they're trying to occupy a space already being held by another church. And without their budget or track record, they don't have a shot. Prospective guests offer no regard for a church plant's potential. They only see it as it is.

Church planting is not just a spiritual or theological undertaking. It's also a sociological one. Even the business community has to face this reality. The grocery chain, Kroger, for example, says it will not open stores in communities where it can't hold the number one or number two positions in the grocery market. The same is true for churches. You won't have much success with a seeker-model church in South Barrington, Illinois. Why bother trying to plant a church focused on creativity in Grapevine, Texas? And forget about a purpose-driven church in Orange County, California. If people are going to attend those kinds of churches, they'll choose the best ones.

To have the most success as a church plant, look for what is not represented in a community and do that! Your gifts and your passions have to line up with what the community needs. But if you feel called to replicate someone else's approach in your town or city, you're going to have a difficult time. The goal is to identify the unique role God wants your church plant to fulfill. Because they all do. And if you're an outsider, if you're not indigenous, you're going to have an even harder time figuring out what that is.

If you're like I was, a parachute planter, there are two ways you can figure out what your role is. One is by making mistake after mistake until you realize what will most impact a community. The other is by waiting as long as you can before you plant the church, and go Jane Goodall on your city. Watch it. Study it. And learn from it before you make a move.

Do What Others Aren't Doing

Mclean Bible Church is the reigning megachurch in northern Virginia. With seven campuses and more than thirteen thousand people in attendance, no other church can hold a candle to what they do well. If you move to Mclean, Virginia, with the hopes of starting a megachurch, you're in for a long and difficult journey. They're already fifty years and millions of dollars ahead of you.

But there's an interesting reason MBC has mastered a few key areas of ministry. Early on, senior pastor Lon Solomon decided to look at what no one other church was doing in northern Virginia and then do exactly that. Years ago no one else was doing young adult ministry in the DC area, so they put their money and resources into what is now a premiere young adult ministry in the country, let alone northern Virginia. No one else was doing ministry for disabled kids, so they captured the market with decided energy.

And no one else was doing video-venue campuses, which they are currently launching at great expense all over the DC area. Mclean Bible decided to do what no one else was doing, to reach people no one else was reaching, and to do it better than anyone else.

It's hard to swallow the idea of churches competing for the same people. It's a reality I hated too. Year after year at Reston, we continued to lose people to other congregations because they did something better than us in one area or another. For one family it was the teaching. I wanted to focus on reaching lost people, not educating Christians. For another family it was liturgy. Ours simply wasn't formal enough. And for those who were struggling with addictive behaviors, I wasn't the deliverer of mercy and guidance they needed. Now I could have protested our attrition problem and gotten angry at the other churches who "stole" our people. But what I needed most was to identify our unique purpose and unashamedly, unabashedly, and unapologetically do that.

Finding Your Niche

God has a specific purpose for every church that gets planted. So when we assume our job is to reach everyone, we never understand why people leave. If we're trying to be something we're not, we not only won't do it well, but we'll come across as a cheap imitation of the other churches that do. Let me go out on a limb here. If God has called you to plant a church, it's because he knows you'll reach different people through different methods than anyone else. You will not only attract people with this distinctive purpose, but you will turn some away. In fact, you'll probably lose more people than you'll keep. But at least you'll be faithful to the purpose for which God has called you.

So how do you find your distinct purpose as a church? Here are some key questions to ask:

- Who are you passionate about reaching? *AR 20-40K*
- If money wasn't a concern, what would your church look like? *modern museum with T.Vis, etc.*
- If denomination wasn't a factor, what would your church look like?
- What kinds of people does God bring into your life?
- What kinds of churches are already thriving in your community? *Oasis, Destiny, Faith Christ?*
- Who is not already being reached?

Think of Your Church as an Idea

Stretch with me on this: think of your new church as an idea for the community. Don't think about the mission and theology for a minute. Just focus on the idea of your church, its way of doing ministry, the needs it's meeting, the people it's attracting. Is it a good idea or a bad idea for the community? How do you know? Ask yourself this question: is the idea spreading?

If it's not, you may not have a spiritual problem. You may have an idea problem. Maybe your church's purpose is not distinguishable enough. Maybe you're not meeting a need in the community. Maybe you're answering questions nobody's asking.

Niches in the New Testament

A lot of us are guilty of reading about the New Testament church with naïveté. We like to think that every church planted throughout the book of Acts looked exactly like every other church. But if you take a closer look, you'll begin to see some unique and distinguishing identities emerge.

Here are a few examples of how some New Testament churches differed from each other:

A Gathering of Givers

Look at how Paul describes the church at Philippi in 2 Corinthians 8:1–2: "We want you to know, brothers, about the grace of God granted to the churches of Macedonia: during a severe testing by affliction, their abundance of joy and their deep poverty overflowed into the wealth of their generosity."

The Philippian church was a giving church in spite of their poverty. They gave money to Paul on numerous occasions, and Paul didn't take money from many of his churches. He couldn't trust that their motives were pure or that they wouldn't come back to accuse him later on. But the Philippians had pure motives.

Fact-Checkers

The Berean church, on the other hand, must have consisted of a colony of teachers. Look at the way Luke describes them as a group in Acts 17:11: "The people here were more open-minded than those in Thessalonica, since they welcomed the message with eagerness and examined the Scriptures daily to see if these things were so."

Since I'm not a detail-oriented person, it would have agonized me to pastor the Bereans. There was nothing wrong with the Bereans, and there was everything right with them. But if they were second-guessing Paul, I'm pretty sure I would've been a bad fit.

Living a Local Vision

Let's make an agreement. If we're going to plant churches, let's plant the churches our communities need, not the ones in our heads. If we're going to start new congregations, we should not only know our demographics but our ecclesiolographics as well. When we survey the community for meeting locations, outreach venues, and target audiences, we should also take stock of what God has been doing through other churches. God doesn't call us to be redundant. He calls us to fulfill a unique and distinguishing vision. If we don't consider the work of other pastors and other churches, we'll never understand why God has called us there.

One of my greatest moments in church planting happened while I was saying good-bye to our church plant. A group of local pastors had come together at my invitation to help me transition RCC to my associate pastor. In their opening remarks, they applauded us for pursuing the unique purpose of our church. We were meeting in a movie theater in the center of our town, and they were incredibly complimentary about what we were doing. They said we were on the front lines, that we were reaching people they could never reach, that we had great courage. I was humbled by the experience because these were all highly accomplished pastors. But indeed, each of their churches was carrying out a different purpose from ours.

Blue Ocean Church

In the book *Blue Ocean Strategy*, authors W. Chan Kim and Renee Mauborgne describe a new way of thinking about business markets. Whereas red oceans are established markets where scores of competitors battle one another over price and negligible benefits for the same customers, blue

oceans are new markets that have no competition.[1] Cirque
du Soleil created a blue ocean. Starbucks created a blue
ocean. And Apple created some products that compete with
practically no one. It's not outlandish to think of our church-
planting strategies in these terms. If you're going to plant a
church, make it so different, unusual, and distinctive that
you are competing with no one else. When you're starting
from scratch and you're trying to plant a church, you can't
afford to compete with anyone else.

Be unapologetic about the kind of church God has called
you to plant. Even if you don't like the idea of *kinds* of
churches, they exist anyway, so you might as well embrace it.
Marketers do. They know they'll suffer if they share their
identity with someone else. So have an identity; know your
identity; fit your identity. And even though you might turn
off some people by your vision, you'll also attract raving loy-
alists, people who have been waiting for a church like yours
to come along. And when they do, you can cast a compelling
vision to expand the movement.

Here's how to cast that vision.

Notes

1. W. Chan Kim and Renée Mauborgne, *Blue Ocean Strategy*
(Harvard Business School Publishing Company, 2005).

13

SPIRITUAL DNA

A Spiritual Identity

By the end of my first job in ministry, I was frustrated with the church. I had been working on staff at a large, traditional church for several years, and the bureaucracy was killing me. I was expected to be in my office during business hours, and if I did any relational work, it had to be done on my own time in addition to the fifty-plus hours I was already working. It seemed like every decision had to pass through a committee or a staff meeting. Evangelism was defined as knocking on doors. An elder once demanded audio playback on a baptism I conducted to make sure I said the correct words: "In the name of the Father, the Son, and the Holy Spirit." One week I was reprimanded for not singing during a worship service. And this was my first official staff job at a church. Needless to say, I was becoming disillusioned.

I was at a crossroads. I either had to walk away, or my soul was going to shrivel up. I went to work every day with a dark cloud hanging over me, a sadness. I knew there had to be something better. This wasn't the kind of ministry I signed up for. I had quit a great job in advertising to impact the world for Christ, and this certainly couldn't be it. Occasionally a fellow staffer noticed my disposition and asked if I was doing OK. I'd mutter something about the heavy workload or late-night movies, but I was having a hard time getting out of bed in the mornings.

A Frustrated Cupbearer

Do you remember the story of Nehemiah? He was a cup-bearer to the Persian king Artaxerxes. When he learned of Jerusalem's destruction, he carried out his tasks with great sadness, posing an incredible risk to his own well-being. Nehemiah 2:1 says that his face was so sullen that the king finally asked him what was bothering him. I remember feeling this way. In fact, this is why I wasn't singing in that particular worship service. And the "king" finally confronted me.

During this time God opened my eyes to the world of church planting. I'd never heard of it before. *You mean, we're allowed to start new churches?* One afternoon in the secrecy of my office, I called a church planting leader in Colorado to find out how much it paid.

"How much it pays?" he replied.

Question answered.

But then I started seeing more and more church planters featured in my denomination's monthly publications. I'm sure they were there all along, but it took some holy frustra-tion for me actually to notice them. One of the planters hap-pened to be my friend Eric from seminary, whom I mentioned earlier. I immediately called him to learn everything I could about church planting. It was like a cloud-parting epiphany. If I didn't like my church's particular way of doing ministry, I didn't have to walk away from the church altogether. I could, in fact, change the paradigm by starting a new church. I could actually reach a whole new people group with a church that matched their culture.

God Uses Frustration to Shape a Vision

Something I didn't realize at the time is that God uses frustration to shape a vision. This is what he did to Nehemiah. And this is what he did to me. If God doesn't build up a tremendous amount of frustration within us, we'll never have the passion to pursue his calling. Planting a church is tough work, but when you go through a long season of frustration, it's a welcome relief from the inner turmoil you've been experiencing.

Prospective church planters have a difficult time understanding the gift of frustration. I know I did. I was losing faith in the church; I was getting upset with my leaders at the injustices, the mindless traditions, and the bureaucracy. But vision was birthed out of my frustration. Clarity and insight were born out of my turmoil. These were gifts from God. The challenge was recognizing what God was doing and not walking away.

Unfortunately many church plants are started out of spite. They're started by church planters who can no longer tolerate their senior leaders. They start a church like a rogue band member would start a garage band, but they can only go as far as their anger will take them. They don't realize that frustration is God's mechanism for igniting passion and vision. Frustration is the fuel that gets them through difficult times. And besides, "getting back at my pastor" doesn't make for a very good mission statement.

So what's frustrating you? What do you complain about?

What You Complain About

Here's an insight I hope will change your life:

What you complain about reveals your gifts.

In other words, you're noticing injustices, inefficiencies, gaps, and abuses in ministry because God has uniquely wired you to do something about them. It may not happen right away. It can take a while for the right conditions to fall into place. You'll notice in Nehemiah that several months go by between chapter 1 where he hears about Jerusalem's destruction and chapter 2 when he can finally talk about it with the king. As Henry Blackaby says, a calling is an invitation to prepare. When the time is right, God will open the door.

Defining Your Vision by What You're Not

I am not a hype man or a hooper.

We should be able to define our church plants not only by what they are but also by what they aren't. This is the part of vision that takes courage. It's not the rallying of people and the casting of vision that requires fortitude; it's resisting the temptation to become all things to all people. *But didn't Paul say we should become all things to all people so we can reach some?* If our role was apostolic like Paul's, then yes. If our job was to carry the gospel to different cultures, then, yes. As missionaries, we're meant to adapt the form of church and meet people where they are. When Paul was in Greece, he was all Greek. When he was in the synagogue, he was all

Jewish. And when he was standing in an Athenian temple, he was a philosopher who could quote the famous poets of the day.

God gives our church plants a unique identity within each community so that we can reach particular people in a particular subculture. God reaches all people through this mosaic of spiritual expressions. The gospel is unifying, but our forms of church are not. I've attended highly popular church services that I could hardly tolerate. Not every form of church is for everyone. So living out our unique identity is how we reach different people. We become a kind of church that spreads throughout a particular kind of culture.

Unapologetic Identity

No matter how biblical we think our approaches are, they are largely shaped around our personal preferences. And that's OK. We have to get comfortable with the fact that we cannot reach everyone. Let me be as clear as I can be. We have to be OK with people leaving our churches. I'll be honest with you: a whole lot more people leave than stay.

Can you be OK with that?

The challenge is that when people leave, they often say it's because we're failing in some area, which makes us feel horrible. We don't have a big enough youth group. Our preaching doesn't feed them. The music is too loud. The sermon is too long. Everyone has a reason for leaving. And if we don't have a clear picture of our purpose, their complaining can easily destroy us.

I don't think we should ignore everyone's parting shots because God could use them to speak truth to us. But if people are leaving because they don't like our vision, we should celebrate. Their exodus verifies that our purpose is being lived out. Vision is affirmed not only by the kind of people we attract but also by the kind of people who leave.

Victims of Circumstance

Without a clear, unapologetic vision we become victims of circumstance. You've seen these kinds of church planters. They're unhappy with the worship music, the quality of their leaders, and the unrelated programs that have been added to the church's calendar. *How did the weekday preschool come to be such a significant part of the church's ministry?* But these circumstances didn't just happen. The leaders failed to navigate these decisions with a clear vision. A vision becomes the filter through which every decision passes.

Just Say No

When I think about uncompromised vision, I think of Vince Antonucci who started Forefront Church in Virginia Beach, Virginia. Vince tells the story of how he wanted Forefront to be a church that reached lost people from day one. He felt he had enough believers in his core group and wanted to attract unbelievers so that outreach would become the DNA of the church. This vision was put to the test when a Christian family attended an outreach Vince was holding. The man said, "I feel like God is calling me to come to your church." Vince responded, "Well, he hasn't told me that, and I don't think you should come." That might sound a bit extreme, but Forefront has gone on to become one of the most effective churches I know at reaching people far from God.

Can you withstand the pressure to become something other than your vision? At times the pressure will grow intense, almost too strong for you to bear. But never forget that once you surrender the original picture for your church, it is nearly impossible to go back. Before long you'll be leading a church that doesn't satisfy the reason you were so impassioned to start one. Stand your ground. Be unapologetic about vision. And the purity of your purpose will attract the people God has called you to reach.

Vision for Sale

A well-defined vision could threaten your bank account. How will you stand up to the pressure of crumbling finances? Is your vision for sale? It's easy to sacrifice vision when the money is running low and you could generate revenue by becoming more things to more people. Some visions will always struggle to become self-sustaining. Take, for instance, churches in poor, urban areas or in Third-World countries. Or maybe even a church for surfers along the coast.

If this is you, four options are available:

1. You can become a bivocational church planter.
2. You can appeal to others for outside support.
3. You can try to turn your converts into colaborers.
4. You can pray for a new vision.

The only thing worse than not pursuing your God-given vision is compromising your God-given vision for the sake of cash flow.

Don't let money do this to you.

Go for Broke

We should never let money stop us from pursuing our vision. Whenever church planters run into financial challenges, we tend to downshift our efforts and, consequently, our effectiveness. When tithing is sparse and people are slow to walk through the door, many of us mistakenly go into activity hibernation. This strategy might squeeze out a few more months of survival, but the church's effectiveness comes to a screeching halt. The goal of the church becomes surviving, which is never an inspiring mission. Our vision should be so daring, so audacious that people are either radically opposed to it or moved to be a part of it. Our God-given vision should be such an inspiring goal that it strikes holy fear into the hearts of people. People should say, as Jonathan did in 1 Samuel 14:6, "Perhaps the LORD will help us." This kind of vision is captivating. It requires us to be all in, to go for broke. Sometimes we do fail, but at least we didn't just survive. At least we weren't just a mild irritant to our communities. At least we really did something.

Four Months to Live

Several years ago my friend Steve Swisher took the reins of a struggling core group in Virginia Beach whose planter had left them. The church was hobbling along, functioning in survival mode, when his bookkeeper told him, "This church has just four months to live. Then we run out of cash, and it's all over."

Rather than cut his losses and walk away, Steve asked himself, "What would I do if I had nothing to lose? What decisions would I make if I had only four months to live?" He immediately shut down the church's operations and said good-bye to some divisive and uncommitted people. Then, based on his new understandings of the community, he crafted a new image, changed the church's name, rented a new location, and hired a new worship leader. The most committed people enthusiastically poured themselves into the restart. The church is now reaching their ideal community and has become self-sustaining with 150 people and climbing.

The Kind of Vision That Unites

Effective leaders know how to unite people around vision. When they speak about the vision, people cheer. When they organize projects around the vision, people rally. And when they call for people to make sacrifices, they go the extra mile. Vision is something people want to embrace, but it needs to be compelling. It needs to enthrall them. I learned this lesson early in my church planting career.

As an analytical thinker, I get excited about the multiplicative spread of the gospel. So when I started Reston Community Church, I wrote down the number of small groups we could have in ten years if we only doubled the number of groups each year. To strategy-minded people like me, this goal was exciting. I was genuinely moved by how many people we could reach if we reproduced disciples in small-group environments. So I came up with a mission statement that encapsulated this idea. It was "to make disciples who could make disciples of Jesus Christ." It fit my passions perfectly.

Unfortunately this vision didn't move other people. Sure, they joined our church and strove to become disciple-makers. But it didn't comfort the afflicted or afflict the comfortable. I laid out a clear formula, but it didn't tug at anybody's heartstrings. It was a proposal without any woo. Know this: how we communicate the vision is just as important as the vision itself. People aren't inspired by spreadsheets. They're inspired by changed lives.

Vision as a Mantra

I think we should abandon mission statements. Half of them are recycled from the most popular churches anyway. But even worse, they're stiff, wordy, and no one can remember them. Here are a few mission statements I've come across:

> [Our church] exists to be used by God as he transforms people into disciples of Jesus Christ, here and around the world.

> [Our church] is devoted to sharing the Word of God with the [local] community and communities in the United States and around the world through fellowship, discipleship, and service.

> [Our church] exists to evangelize the lost, edify the saved, minister to those in need, and be a conscience in the community.

They're not bad. But do they incite anything within you? Aren't their words a bit lifeless and benign? I can't exactly see Mel Gibson shouting these mission statements to the ranks of warring Scots who are about to fight England in *Braveheart*. They sound as if lawyers wrote them. In fact, I don't see how they're much distinguished from those of other churches. They have the ring of "We sort of want to do big things for God if he's OK with that." They don't provide the inspiration we need to charge the gates of hell.

Mission statements are like sandbags on a hot air balloon. They're great at keeping the church grounded, but if you want to take off, they don't contribute much. Here's what I think: we should eliminate mission statements altogether and replace them with mantras. Mantras are made up of one to five, maybe six, words that define the church's purpose.

One word is ideal, but that can be tough. Here are some actual mantras that work well:

> Love God. Love People. Prove It.
> Just Jesus.
> Love beyond Reason.
> Change the Story.
> Jesus. Period.

Notice how audacious these mantras feel. They're memorable. They incite passion. And they're active. They'd look great on a shield.

It's not just churches that have caught onto mantras. Political campaigns and businesses know the power of simple phrases as well:

> Ron Paul Revolution.
> We Try Harder.
> It's the Economy, Stupid.
> Think Different.
> Just Do It.

Sticky Mantras

If you can't tattoo the phrase on your forearm, it's too long. The goal here is to create a statement that packs a punch, something people can remember. We're looking for stickiness. A sticky mantra is a highly memorable phrase that carries great power in its simplicity. A sticky mantra can become even more popular than the church's name. A Southern Baptist Church in Duluth, Georgia, calls itself "The Family Church." They use it so much that I honestly don't know the church's real name.

When you come up with a mantra, ask yourself what you want the church to be known for. To create the perfect mantra is not an easy task, but it's worth it. They say that great writing is rewriting, that giving a ten-minute speech is harder than a thirty-minute speech. The same is true for mantras. It's much more difficult to be short and sweet than to write a long, uninteresting mission statement. But it's well worth it. Take a moment to write down the key word or words that define your church's purpose.

_____

_____

_____

_____

_____

_____

_____

_____

Now that you've identified your church plant's unique spiritual DNA, let's move on to how to go about achieving it.

14

ROOT SYSTEMS

Your Vision Is Worthless

Vision has the capability to excite people, unite them, rally them, and compel them to make sacrifices. But without a step-by-step process to achieve it, your vision is worthless. It's like standing up at a baseball game with forty-five thousand other people to yell, "Charge!" only to sit down and resume eating your hotdog. Every plant needs roots, and in a church plant these roots are organizational systems. And yes, even something as spiritual as the church needs systems. Systems are how your church as an organization conducts itself. And as the old saying goes, every organization is perfectly designed to achieve the results it gets.

Everyone Has a System

Whether they admit it or not, every church has a system—even the ones that are an organizational mess. It might not be a good system, but it's still a system. Claiming you don't have a system doesn't make it so. I've heard pastors boast in doing only what's scriptural, nothing pragmatic, but then follow an arduous system to achieve what's scriptural. Refusing to believe in systems for your church doesn't make them nonexistent. Avoiding a system is a system.

A system is the way your organization operates. It's a series of steps that are repeated (or not repeated) as a way of accomplishing your goals. They can be highly organized and intentional, or they can be scattered and disorganized. But systems exist. You just can't easily see them. They're invisible unless you're looking for them. You can have highly organized systems that are bad. And you can have highly disorganized systems that are good (although not very good). But systems run your church and are ultimately what produce your results.

The North Point System

Andy Stanley, the pastor of North Point Community Church in Alpharetta, Georgia, created a powerful illustration about the system that runs his church. In one meeting Andy laid a sheet of paper at one end of the room and said that it represented someone who was far from God. Then he laid another sheet of paper on the other side of the room that represented a fully devoted follower of Jesus. The church's mission, he said, was to turn the first kind of person into the second kind of person. For dramatic effect Andy had several staff members try to jump from one piece of paper to the other, but it was too far. Andy reminded the staff that it would take several steps for someone far from God to become a disciple of Christ. What, then, were the steps needed to help this transformation happen?

The answer for North Point was to create three spiritual environments that would lead people into a closer relationship with others and with God. The environments were called the foyer, the living room, and the kitchen. The idea is that when people come to your house, they start in the foyer. This is where people are welcomed and get to know one another. Then people gravitate to the living room for deeper conversation. And finally guests end up in the kitchen where deep community is happening. To mirror this process, North Point established the worship service as the foyer, midsize groups for the living room, and small groups for the kitchen. This system is expressed through their logo, on their Web site, and in their church's everyday vocabulary.

Create Your System

Creating a system starts with understanding your church's unique vision. Hopefully you've identified your purpose by now and can move onto creating a system that accomplishes it. But the vision must be clear. If it's not, you'll have a hard time developing a system. The system should serve the vision, not the other way around. Sadly many churches carry out meaningless systems simply because it's the way they've always done things. Tradition is valued more than the vision.

Once you can articulate your vision in a mantra, you're ready to create the steps for achieving it. Whom are you trying to reach? What kind of people? What do you want them to become? Now how do you help them make this transformation? This is not as easy as it sounds. You have to consider what it takes to reach these people, what it takes to keep them engaged, and what it looks like to be effective. You'll wrestle long and hard with creating an effective system because what you think will work most often doesn't. As you create a system, you have to remain flexible through the inventing process, willing to change when your plans fail and new insights become available.

Draw It on a Napkin

What are the necessary steps to achieve your church's vision? Now draw it on a napkin. You can make it as simple as a few circles connected by arrows, a funnel, or even a metaphor. Andy Stanley used a household metaphor. Rick Warren used a baseball diamond to illustrate his discipleship process. When I started Reston Community Church, my system looked like a rocket ship.

But a church system doesn't have to be so structured. Mark Batterson of National Community Church created a map with fictitious islands to illustrate his discipleship process. Attendees can move from Seeker Island to Learner Island to Influencer Island to Investor Island in no particular order. Mark's one of the most intuitive pastors I know so he's happy to see people chart their own course.

The point is to have a system people can quickly grasp. They need to be able to see where they fit and understand the milestones. I can already hear the criticism: *How can we turn something as spiritual as discipleship into a formula?* The word *disciple* comes from the word *discipline*. Commitments and disciplines are necessary for spiritual growth, and as each church reaches different people, they use different systems to disciple them.

Take a moment to sketch your church's system:

Leave your rets
Yoke bearing
Cross submitting

_____
_____
_____

Do Nothing Else

Now that you've created a system, do nothing else in your church but that. Your system is the straightest path to achieving your vision so any unrelated activity puts a drag on your effectiveness. Creating a system is just as much about what your church will not do to achieve its mission as it is about what it will do. Once you create the system, it becomes a filter through which all organizational decisions are made. It will keep you from starting unrelated ministries, and it will focus all of your church's efforts on one defined path.

The system then becomes a benchmark for how effective your vision really is. If you're not achieving your vision, it will show you exactly why and in which part of the process. For example, if you're not reaching people in the first place, the rest of the system won't function. Or if your people aren't growing spiritually, the system will show you what step is breaking down. The system will expose any weaknesses in your overall ministry plan and allow you to adjust it piece by piece.

Create an Org Chart

The next step is turning your system into an organizational chart. This is how people engage with the vision of your church. It's how they know where they fit. And it's the best way to steward the spiritual gifts God gives believers. First Corinthians 12:12 says, "For as the body is one and has many parts, and all the parts of that body, though many, are one body—so also is Christ."

That the Bible uses the body as a metaphor for the church is telling. If these body parts don't all come together for one purpose, the result is a crippled church. An organizational chart is the best way for people to see exactly how they support this greater purpose. It orchestrates the church's activity and helps everyone find a role. When I hear people say they don't like organization, what they mean is they don't like organization that doesn't suit them. But people love organization that serves them well. An org chart doesn't constrain people. It liberates them to use their gifts. It emphasizes their values and encourages them to use their abilities. Without them people never know where they stand in the church's mission.

Organize the System into Roles

To create an org chart, start by writing down every conceivable role that's necessary to carry out the system. Don't try to arrange it in any special way just yet, and don't leave anything out, not even the smallest task. Don't forget about the nursery team or the leadership team or even the church treasurer. But avoid the temptation to add a role that doesn't fit your system just because other churches have them.

Now start grouping these roles into ministry areas. Highlight the needed leadership roles as they naturally appear. The important thing is to create an org chart that carries out the system. We're not organizing around personalities in the church. We're organizing around the church's vision and system. This is, after all, the reason God called our churches into existence. If our churches are based on personalities, what happens when those personalities leave?

Role Descriptions

Now that you've written down your vision, your system for accomplishing it, and the org chart that structures it, the next step is to write one-page job descriptions for each role in the organization. This includes not only paid staff but also volunteers. Especially volunteers. You want to ensure that the work of ministry gets done and that everyone is contributing to the same vision. When people have to guess their roles, they'll make up their own visions. Remember, the purpose of creating a system is to become more effective at achieving your vision. If you're going to let people create their own roles, you should start a community center, an Internet chat room maybe, but certainly not a church. The mission God has given you is far too important.

Surprisingly, when we give people role descriptions in the church, they feel liberated. Think about the challenges that keep volunteers from serving:

- They don't know what's expected of them.
- They're afraid of having to serve too much.
- They don't know what success looks like.
- They want to know how they'll benefit.
- They're not sure they can do the task.

Creating role descriptions takes care of all of these concerns. In one document we can spell out exactly what the role entails, the time commitments involved, and instructions on how to exit the role if needed. With a formal document we make the work of ministry objective, not personal. Volunteers often feel like they can never step out of the role unless they leave the church. Role descriptions provide a way for people to replace themselves without the guilt.

Makeup of a Role Description

A role description should start with the overall purpose of the role. For example, a nursery volunteer's description could say: "To provide babies with a nurturing, loving, and safe environment that reflects God's love for children." This purpose sets the tone for how the nursery is arranged, which activities are scheduled, and who is allowed to enter the nursery area. All who volunteer in this ministry are agreeing with this purpose and see it as paramount to their responsibilities. To achieve this goal on Sunday morning is a win for the nursery team.

After the purpose is stated, a job description lists the overall responsibilities of the area. This list includes every task that needs to be performed each time. So, again, in the nursery environment a description can include things like these:

- Arrive by 7:30 a.m. to prepare the nursery environment.
- Arrange the check-in area for parents and set up the signs.
- Join the overall volunteer team to pray together at 8:00 a.m.
- Be prepared to start receiving babies into the nursery by 8:30 a.m.

You can find a complete library of role descriptions at ChurchInTheMaking.com.

Two things to note: First, role descriptions should be one page in length for easier readability. And second, role descriptions can be used as a tool for recruiting volunteers. They help you emphasize the seriousness of the role and its importance to the church's vision. No one will take it seriously if you don't.

Recruiting Volunteers

People don't like to be managed, especially volunteers. They get enough of that five days a week at their jobs. So role descriptions take away the need to manage people and place it on managing agreements. People want volunteering to be a choice, not an obligation. They want to feel appreciated for what they contribute, not taken for granted. And the best way to measure and appreciate someone's contribution is to spell it out. Leaders who think role descriptions will limit a person's contribution are mistaken. Role descriptions simply point people in the right direction. They'll go the extra mile.

When you're recruiting people for a role, ask to meet with them in person. This will underscore the importance of the role. Eventually the leaders of your ministry areas will need to recruit their own volunteers, but you may have to model it first. If you're recruiting someone who is already serving in another area, don't combine the job descriptions. Keep them separate so that the system stays pure. Think of each role in the org chart as a separate entity, deserving of its own focus and priority. This is the only way to build a system in your church that will survive attrition and bailouts. You don't want your church to come to a screeching halt just because someone who is multitalented leaves.

When you meet with recruits, talk through the role description. Explain each responsibility and why it's important to the role. This will undergird your core values as an organization. Also explain how they can replace themselves or step out of the role if necessary. This will help them see it's not a lifetime sentence but that there are on and off ramps if they need them. Ask them if they have any questions. Give them a chance to challenge the process. When you're sure they understand the role and agree to it, tell them why you believe they're right for the role. Affirm their gifts and share how their involvement will fulfill the church's vision. Ask them if they'd like to accept the role. If they say no, thank them for their time and ask if there's a better role for them. But if they're onboard, thank them for accepting and say a prayer to seal the agreement.

From this point on, you are not managing the person; you are managing an agreement. Again, no one likes to be managed. So a role description takes the authority off your shoulders and puts it on the agreement. If volunteers fall short of their role descriptions, you can ask them if they misunderstood the agreement. But you're managing agreements, not people.

A Church That Runs on Systems

At Reston Community Church, we had a strong leader who created a unique role for himself by the sheer force of his personality. It wasn't a bad thing. He loved the church and its vision, but he wasn't contributing directly to the system. So I offered him several roles on the organizational chart that he could fill, and he gladly accepted. His small group and ministry team became wildly popular, but I rested easier knowing that our church's success didn't depend on his personality but on the role he carried out in our system.

A systems-dependent church doesn't sound very spiritual. After all, what if God brings someone extraordinarily gifted to your church? Shouldn't you make room for her gift? Let him start a new ministry? It's certainly tempting. But how much do you care about the vision God gave you? Will you let it be deterred by the popularity of someone's personality? And how will you find a replacement should they ever leave? A personality-dependent church is vulnerable to the whims of people. But a systems-dependent church can withstand these setbacks. Operating on systems doesn't squelch personalities; it just focuses them.

Filling Your Organizational Chart

Every church struggles to fill its organizational chart. I don't know a single church that couldn't use more volunteers. But there's a better way to stream people into your ministry without having to beg them. At Reston Community Church we used three steps for assimilation: the welcome center, the follow-up, and the newcomer's lunch. This system might not work for your church, but it did for ours. At one point we had nearly 90 percent of our regular attendees serving in ministry. Let me explain how it worked.

The Welcome Center

When guests visited our church, we guided them toward an obvious welcome center that was designed to turn them from strangers into friends. We recruited our most hospitable people for this role and let them put their gifts into action. At the welcome center we invited visitors to sign our guest book, which was literally a guest book. We found that people were more likely to sign a guest book than to fill out a visitor card. It just seemed safer to them.

The Follow-up

We followed up with a handwritten note that next week and then a phone call from me. I never asked for anything; I simply thanked them for coming. We allowed the guests to enjoy reasonable anonymity for two weeks and then asked small group leaders to make contact. Again this was an intentional system spelled out in the role descriptions. The small group leaders were encouraged to send a casual e-mail, inviting guests to their groups. We knew that if guests joined a small group, they would be more likely to stick around. But most important, we invited guests to attend a once-a-month newcomer's lunch.

The Newcomer's Lunch

We held a newcomer's lunch on the last Sunday of every month and announced it every week in the Sunday service. Not every guest would come the first time, but the beauty of it was they only had to wait four weeks before the next one came along. We hosted it in the back room of a nearby restaurant and made it as casual as possible. We got to know one another for the first twenty minutes, and then I talked about the vision of the church for about ten minutes. After sharing our vision and values, I described how each person in our church made the vision possible. I then explained how they could be a part of it and offered response cards where they could indicate their interest. Some people were ready to serve right away; others wanted to attend a partnership class (or membership class) first.

The Beauty of Systems

A church's system doesn't have to be impersonal. Think about Starbucks. They have a finely tuned system for running their stores. Their employees must hit sales goals and adhere to dress codes. Someone in their Seattle headquarters even selects the art on the walls. Yet the atmosphere at Starbucks feels remarkably casual and personal. The same goes for your church.

A system doesn't have to be impersonal. It simply has to carry out your vision. Coming up with a system will force you to kill your sacred cows and identify your true purpose for existing. I imagine this exercise will frustrate you to no end. It'll show you some things about yourself that you don't like. But creating a system will change your church. It will inspire your people and produce results. It's a stewardship. To use your best strategic thinking is to make the most of the resources with which God has entrusted you.

Then you will see the fruit of your labor.

15

MUCH FRUIT

The Result of a System

Something remarkable happens when you design a church to run on systems rather than personalities. It becomes reproducible. To be clear, the church doesn't *have to* reproduce. It doesn't have to plant other churches or start multisite campuses or launch video venues. It can simply exist on its own for as long as it likes. But when a church moves away from personalities and focuses on systems, the church becomes primed and ready to multiply. The vision becomes the focus, which can be replicated in other locations.

You can reproduce a church without systems, but I don't recommend it. Starting from scratch is no fun. You begin with no momentum, no continuity, and you have a long season of trial and error ahead of you. What is wisdom but learning from other people's mistakes? If I'm advocating anything in this book, it's that successful church planting spills over from momentum, spiritual or otherwise. If you're starting from scratch, you're either called to be a missionary (until a church can be planted), or you've overlooked the church God was nurturing around you. Either way you've got your work cut out for you.

Learning from the Best

Every time I go out to eat with my family at Cracker Barrel, I marvel. I'm not a Southerner, mind you. I don't like grits or biscuits and gravy. Food that claims I'll "slap my momma" is a turnoff. And I have an aversion to country knickknacks and hand-sewn wall hangings. But I'm astonished by the systems of the Cracker Barrel restaurant chain. All of their locations, which are conveniently located off highway exits, feature the same down-home ambiance. In cool weather there's always a warm fire crackling in the dining room's fireplace. The gift shop is loaded with nostalgic games and goodies for the kids. And the seating areas are separated by the same gray latticework in all of its restaurants. Rocking chairs line the front porch in order to help diners wait comfortably for their tables. If it weren't for the fact that all of the restaurants look the same, you'd think a loving grandmother with the gift of hospitality decorated each one. Cracker Barrel has a remarkable system for reproducing restaurants, and that's why they reproduce everywhere with relative ease.

Before you assume I'm advocating that all churches look the same, let me clarify something. We cannot remove the human factor from a church. No matter how great our systems, personalities will always determine the defining characteristics of a church. This is precisely what God intends. Just as Paul's personality and Peter's personality are clearly evident in their respective epistles, so our local churches reflect our unique identities as well. But the systems make a church sustainable and reproducible. All of us in ministry have been highly influenced by the leaders who went before us, even the churches we attended growing up. And no matter how hard we try to change, we reproduce many of these characteristics in our own churches. We can't get away from our pasts.

Creating systems is a more intentional way to reproduce the work of ministry. It allows us to perpetuate best practices. These are the best ways of doing things. And that's a stewardship of effectiveness.

Spiritual Franchising

I don't like comparing the church to a restaurant franchise. The church is a supernatural entity, the body of Christ, the manifest presence of God on the earth. But hear me out. The idea of franchising, or reproducing systems, was God's idea long before McDonald's or Cracker Barrel came along. Just look at what Paul instructed Timothy to do in 2 Timothy 2:2: "And what you have heard from me in the presence of many witnesses, commit to faithful men who will be able to teach others also."

Call it what you like—discipleship, mentoring, or personal coaching—but this is the practice of spiritual franchising. It's the idea of placing the gospel in a system of transfer that won't break down. Without such a plan the gospel's continuity is left to a few spiritual entrepreneurs or apostolic leaders to reintroduce their generation to Jesus. But the plan for the gospel was to travel through every generation by way of systems. The church was never meant to be the point of the gospel, but rather the gospel was meant to be the point of the church. In other words, the gospel doesn't exist to support the church, but the church exists to support the gospel. So the idea of creating a system (namely the church) to perpetuate the gospel is exactly what God had in mind.

Spiritual franchising is already happening. Each generation of pastors is learning from the one before it, whether it's through direct mentoring or even books and conferences. The names of our churches reflect this learning. How many churches named after trees and rivers do you know that have been inspired by Willow Creek? Or how many church planting networks do you know that are springing up around one iconic leader? The whole multisite movement is based on the idea that if you've got a good thing going on, then reproduce it.

Since we're already engaged in spiritual franchising, we might as well be intentional about it. How do we do this? Pay attention to what works in our churches, document it, create a system, and then empower people to do it. Rather than looking at ourselves as leaders that no one can replace, we should look at our leadership role apart from our personalities and figure out how others could do our job. The gospel depends on it.

The Obstacles of Reproduction

The trouble is we've introduced a number of obstacles that make it difficult to reproduce our churches. We ignore the systems that are badly needed to reach more people with the gospel. Here are five obstacles that keep us from reproducing churches:

Barrier 1: Pride

Replacing ourselves requires humility. That's why most pastors don't do it. We love the idea that no one could do what we do. We adore the feeling of being irreplaceable. And even when we believe in the idea of empowering others, we fall short in practice because what then would we do? After all, we've worked our whole lives to achieve this level of success, this position of influence. Why would we hand it off to someone else? Just look at how effective we are.

As we read through the accounts of great leaders in the Bible, one thing is clear: God doesn't hesitate to replace his prophets. He raises up new voices for new generations. Let me put this another way. You can either replace yourself, or God will do it for you. But it's much more admirable and rewarding to be an empowering leader. It just takes humility to see your situation as God sees it.

One of my favorite personalities in the Bible is Barnabas. He was known as a man of encouragement, he was accomplished, he was successful. And he was the rightful apostle to carry the gospel into the ancient world. But then a young punk named Paul came along who had a radical salvation experience on the road to Damascus. Paul had been a terror to the church world, invading homes, arresting innocent people, and even involved in killing Christians. If there was anyone who didn't deserve to be an apostle, it was Paul.

But Barnabas saw the very thing that God had seen in Paul—someone who, if unleashed, could turn the world on its head for the cause of Christ. And so Barnabas, at the risk of great peril to his personal career, replaced himself. He encouraged Paul to take his place, and the rest is history. Barnabas took a backseat in the remaining biblical accounts. But something tells me that Paul won't be the only acclaimed hero in heaven. Humility seems to mean an awful lot to God.

In a world where pastors strive to keep up with one another's successes, it's rare to find an example of this kind of humility. However, last year on a trip to Memphis, I found one. Five years ago a Caucasian pastor named John Bryson had planted a church called Fellowship Bible Church in downtown Memphis to reach the racially divided community that makes up this city. Memphis was where schools had a long history of segregation, where Martin Luther King Jr. was assassinated. Needless to say, it would take a tremendous amount of love to build a truly multicultural church.

Several years ago John recognized that if they were going to succeed at this, he needed to replace himself with an African-American pastor. So he found an amazing preacher and leader named Bryan Lorrits to take his job. But rather than leave the church, John stayed on staff, with his strong business acumen and encouragement, to support the new pastor. Today the church is reaching more than twelve hundred people each week with a remarkable level of diversity.

Barrier 2: Personality

Some of the personalities you'll find in the pastorate are irreplaceable, let alone unforgettable. When I was a kid, my children's pastor was a Barnum & Bailey–trained circus clown. He could tell Bible stories with the same excitement as Saturday morning cartoons and then tie off a complicated balloon animal in sixty seconds to drive a point home. He organized vacation Bible schools that rivaled town festivals. He performed magic tricks in the church lobby and impersonated every celebrity that a kid cares about. But then one year this pastor left our church, and the children's ministry had to start all over again. There were no systems, no instructions; and there certainly wasn't anyone to take his place.

Outrageous personalities in the church are not bad. In fact, they're wonderful. But without systems to guide them, we're setting ourselves up for a fall. If the pastor goes away, does the church go away? When one staff member leaves, does her ministry area have to be reinvented by the next hire? Or does each new leader perpetuate the purposes and systems of the church? By putting personality ahead of purpose, we make our churches difficult to reproduce, let alone sustain.

I earlier mentioned Rock Harbor Church in Costa Mesa, California. Several months ago I met Mike Erre who is a teaching pastor there. At first I thought this meant he taught on Wednesday nights or occasionally filled in for the pastor. But when I asked him about his role in the church, I was surprised to learn that he actually speaks most Sunday mornings. The lead pastor, Todd Proctor, takes a less visible role in the church. I was blown away when I heard this. I don't know many senior pastors who would give up 50 percent of their time in the pulpit, let alone most of the time. Mike explained that he, too, was starting to share the teaching with other pastors on staff. They didn't want people to become too dependent on one personality. In effect, Rock Harbor has created a system whereby the gospel is perpetuated from generation to generation without anchoring it on themselves. They've created a reproducible model of church at the expense of their own egos.

Barrier 3: Professionalism

The church can only reproduce itself when the barriers to leadership are sufficiently reduced for ordinary, unprofessional ministers. Thankfully Jesus did this on the cross when the temple veil that represented the separation of the Spirit of God from humankind was ripped from top to bottom. From that day on, those who placed their faith in Jesus' substitutionary atonement became members of the royal priesthood. Like it or not, we don't need to go to seminary or understand Greek or have an occupational calling to lead a church. Just look at Jesus' disciples: they were rabbinical school dropouts. In fact, their ordinary credentials made them more likely candidates for spiritual greatness. Yet look at how many churches keep the barriers high for church leadership. And I'm not talking about biblical qualifications but rather academic ones. Unfortunately we hinder the movement of the gospel by making aspiring world changers jump through unnecessary hoops.

John Wesley is my favorite reformer from modern church history. He took the role of preacher and made it accessible to the common man. And rightfully so. He knew that reproducing the church meant reducing the barriers that professional clergy had constructed to heighten their own honor. Wesley would gather tobacco farmers in a local barn and preach five to six sermons in one sitting. The farmers would take copious notes and then go back to their own communities to preach these same sermons. Imagine what would have happened if Wesley had insisted that he preach all of his own messages. He never would have impacted as many people, and he would have deprived generations and generations of Methodists from serving God in a substantial way. Wesley knew the importance of deprofessionalizing ministry and using systems to empower leaders.

While attending Pastor Mark Dever's weekender for young pastors last year, I was amazed to see that he had trained and empowered more than fifty men in his congregation to preach within a week's notice. I'm pretty sure none of these men are farmers or fishermen; they're likely Capitol Hill staffers, attorneys, and corporate executives. But not many of them are seminary graduates either. They willingly joined a process that empowered them to become churchmen. Mark Dever took the professional requirements out of leadership so that the gospel could be multiplied.

Community Christian Church in Naperville, Illinois, has developed a simple pathway to help marketplace leaders transition into ministry leadership. Community pastor Jon Ferguson explained that apprenticeships are the key to producing more campus pastors and church planters within their network. A small group leader can become a coach, who can then become a director on staff, and finally a campus pastor or church planter. CCC currently has nine campuses with plans to add eight more in the next two years.

Barrier 4: Excellence in Ministry

We honor God when we give our absolute best in ministry, but excellence is too often a substitute for authentic and relational ministry. It's much easier for a church to build a coffee shop in its lobby than to have all of its members invite newcomers over for dinner. Today, in some of our more forward-thinking churches, there isn't much difference between the technology you see in worship services and what you see at a high-end rock show. How in the world do you reproduce that?

I'm not being critical of using high-end technology. But I wonder if this is really what it means for the church to progress. Was this the great missing puzzle piece from the early church's effectiveness? Dare I say it, but from a historical and global perspective, I'd say the church does best when excellence isn't even relevant. You don't think about quality musicians when you're having church in an underground cellar because the threat of arrest or persecution is high. Yet the church seems to grow faster and with more purity in these circumstances.

There's another reason excellence poses a problem. Quality at its highest levels is almost impossible to reproduce. The cost of doing ministry becomes so high that few others have the means to replicate it.

Let me give you a bad example. My wife, Ainsley, is a distributor for a multilevel marketing company. It's more recreational for her than occupational; she's a big fan of the organic products and nutritional supplements she sells. But to help her become more productive at building her business, we've read up on multilevel sales techniques. One of the principles in recruiting people to work with you is to keep it simple. For example, holding meetings in hotel ballrooms is too expensive for others to replicate, so you don't do it. Even showing a sales presentation with a video projector can keep some people from getting involved. So whatever you do, ensure that anyone else can do it too.

When it comes to the greatest multilevel marketing message in the world—the gospel—are we ensuring its reproducibility? Are we keeping the entry costs low enough to ensure that others can share it too?

Hear me out. I think the quality of our church services could use some healthy sabotage right about now. That's right, I said sabotage. So we don't use a professional graphic designer to create our bulletins, and someone leaves. One thing I love about the story of Jesus entering Jerusalem on a donkey is that the crowd was split over the spectacle. Half of the people saw the fulfillment of messianic prophecy. But the other half was jeering him: "A king on a donkey?" Jesus seemed to sabotage his own ministry on a number of occasions with tactics that sifted people's motives. He wasn't trying to build a ministry that no one could emulate. Excellence would have meant riding into town on a stallion. But Jesus was about to hand off his ministry to a bunch of ragamuffins who would probably ride donkeys.

Barrier 5: Personal Legacy

I'm in the conference-making business. I started a one-day event called The Whiteboard Sessions, and I currently produce an experience called STORY. It's my job to assess what makes events successful and why some conferences struggle. I'll give you an inconvenient truth. Many struggling conferences were started by people who simply wanted to put themselves on a platform. When you hear stories of great men and women of God who amass thousands of people to hear them speak, it makes you, quite selfishly, want the same thing. Who doesn't want God to bless their own ministry? The trouble comes when we try to create our own personal legacies rather than letting God do it.

A big reason churches don't create systems is because the pastor is too busy trying to build a legacy. Many leaders don't trust God for their platforms, but try to build them on their own power. Trying to become a great leader can get in the way of a reproducible church. It's amazing how many church planters came from churches that underestimated their potential. Senior pastors are notorious for underestimating the potential of their staff, mostly because they overestimate their own potential. Creating systems in your church is a far better way to leave a legacy than building up yourself. If God wants you to become an iconic leader, the platforms and opportunities will come to you.

Give It Away

When you're starting a church, this may not be the statement you want to hear. But the point of planting a church is to give it away. When you're starting a new congregation, your passion is strong and your commitment is high. But church planting can burn you out. When people leave, you will be devastated. And make no mistake about it; they will leave. You'll experience months of nail-biting as finances run low and bills keep pouring in. You'll experience seasons of stress as division threatens your unity. You'll have bad services and good services, high points and low points. You'll pray for more leaders and work hard to reach your community. And there will be times when you'll wish you had never done it.

But it will be worth it. You will reach people who would have never been reached otherwise. You'll see God respond to your faith and provide in ways you couldn't have imagined. Christ will become more real to you than ever before, and your relationship with him will be stretched and strengthened like nothing else. Most important, you will see that God did it all. He's the one who builds his church and does a new work in you and impacts your community forever.

And this is precisely why you must give it away.

It's not your church. No matter how much of the burden you bear upon your shoulders or how much you personally sacrifice, it's not your congregation. You are simply a tool God uses to expand his kingdom. Give it away because this is how you empower the next generation of leaders. Give it away because the kingdom doesn't depend on you as much as you think it does. Give it away because your own family needs more of you. Give it away because the church needs a succession plan. Give it away because tomorrow is promised to no one.

Systems are the only way you can give away your church: systems that equip other leaders, systems that run the church without you, and systems that can survive the loss of key people. If you build these systems into your church from the beginning, you'll never worry about whether the church will survive.

When I left Reston Community Church, I had effectively worked myself out of a job. In fact, part of me was slightly embarrassed that the church didn't skip a beat when I left. I didn't want them to think I wasn't working hard enough. But the truth was that our systems had raised up strong leaders. I had given away our church long before I walked away from it.

The Gospel Depends on It

The fruit of the gospel comes from building a church that can exist without you and beyond you. Jesus spent three intense years with his disciples giving them a system. The reason he did this was because the gospel depended on a system to reach the next generation. "As the Father has sent Me, I also send you" (John 20:21), he said. Jesus knew he wouldn't be around to do the work of ministry, so he had to create a system that his disciples could carry out.

Notice that the Great Commission is to "make disciples," not converts. Only disciples can reproduce themselves. Discipleship is the commitment to a system. Jesus had so much faith in the principle of reproducibility that he entrusted the salvation of the entire world to twelve—make that eleven—disciples. And it's truly amazing that by giving away his work of ministry, greater things were accomplished than if he had tried to do everything himself.

Your church plant is the continuation of this Great Commission. You are called not only to start a church to reach your community but also to reach future generations. How will you set up your church to accomplish this? How will you reach people in the future that you will never meet? How will you equip and empower the church leaders of the future? God has been preparing a church around you for this purpose. It's your job to discover it . . . this church in the making.

QUESTIONS FROM PART 3

Foreign Fields

1. How do you create a church that can survive the loss of key people?
2. What is your vision for the church? Is it a vision with which your community is pregnant, or are you inflicting it upon them?
3. What would it mean for you to be a missionary rather than a church planter?
4. Who around you has become committed to you and your vision?
5. How do you launch a church out of the community?

Challenge: Make a list of all the people who owe you their spiritual lives to one degree or another. Identify the people whose faith in Christ you have nurtured. Now examine whether there's a church in the making here.

Indigenous Plants

1. What kinds of people does God naturally bring into your life?

2. Is your church a "good idea" for your community? If so, is it spreading?
3. If money weren't a consideration, what would your church plant look like?
4. What kinds of churches are already thriving in your community?
5. What kinds of people are not already being reached?

Challenge: Describe the kind of people your church is most likely to reach and, more important, the kind of people you'll likely turn away.

Spiritual DNA

1. How has God used frustration to shape a vision in you?
2. What are your frustrations with the church?
3. How do these frustrations possibly reveal your gifts?
4. How has uncompromised vision already made you a victim of circumstance?
5. How has money affected your vision? Have you been tempted to sell out?

Challenge: Scrap your church's mission statement. Write down a simple but powerful mantra that defines your church's purpose. Does this inspire people?

Root Systems

1. What steps are necessary to achieve your church's vision?
2. What metaphor could you use to illustrate your system?
3. What traditions have been getting in the way of your system?

4. Why might it be difficult for you to create role descriptions for volunteers?
5. How is your church plant more dependent on personalities than systems?

Challenge: Once you create an organizational chart out of your system, start by writing a one-page role description for one of your volunteers. Use this as a model for how you will create all of them.

Much Fruit

1. What is the biggest obstacle you face in reproducing yourself?
2. If your church were designed to be a franchise, what would it look like?
3. What influences from your past have you already repeated in your own life?
4. How would you lead your church differently if the point was to give it away?
5. How will you set up your church to reach future generations beyond your lifetime?

Challenge: Ask God to change how you see your role as a church planter. Rather than building a church to further your own legacy, pray for the courage and the humility to empower future church leaders, to give it all away.

CONCLUSION

Despite the number of new churches that either flounder or fail, we continue to start them year after year in the same exact same way. It's like watching Revolutionary War soldiers go to battle against the redcoats by standing in line formation. Why weren't they trained to duck? It was war after all. I feel the same frustration with church planting. Why do we continue sending planters out to the field by themselves with no momentum, very little support, and the odds stacked against them? It's a spiritual war, after all.

We do it because we believe that church planting is a holy mystery. We do our best to assess the planter's spiritual beliefs and personal competency, but we don't really believe the results are knowable. When a new church flourishes, we say, "God is just blessing." And when it fails, we chalk it up to a botched assessment. It never dawns on us that a new church's success or failure is determined long before it ever starts.

My prayer is that this book will change how churches are planted.

A new church needs spiritual fertility to thrive. A hardened community has to be cultivated for the seed of the gospel to take root. Until then, church planters get stuck in a spin cycle of fruitless activity. In this context they have to do the work of a missionary. They have to build relationships, heal emotional wounds, and lower the walls of spiritual resistance through prayer and consistent testimony. When good ground finally emerges, the planter will start to see fruit from his efforts. He can assemble a congregation of believers, but only after the work of cultivation. Otherwise, the mission gets lost in the grind of building an organization. Tasks such as forming small groups and updating the Web site get in the way of the church's primary task—reaching lost people for Christ.

A new church also needs social momentum to thrive. This comes by starting churches out of other churches so they don't become charities in and of themselves. A church started with momentum easily breaks through critical mass and becomes socially validated by the size of its core group. Anything less, and guests will always wonder if something's wrong. They'll be cordial, even complimentary, but they won't come back. It's no coincidence that some of the most effective church plants were started by former youth pastors, collegiate ministers, and hometown heroes. God uses the relationships they groomed over the years to spark new congregations. These church planters don't have to sell people on the new church; they mobilize them.

And finally, a new church needs deep roots in the community to thrive. This means being indigenous to the community, shaping a homegrown vision, and gathering a team of loyal partners. As long as the planter is an outsider, his community will always hold him suspect. It can take years for him to not only act and think like a local, but to be accepted by them. When the planter is already leading people in the community, there's no need to sell the vision of the church. They've already lived it. And now they want to help others experience the same life transformation. New churches with deep roots grow quickly because the vision has already been validated and the church planter has been proven.

We've somehow come to view church planting as something similar to launching a retail store. We conduct demographic studies, prepare marketing campaigns, and plan for the grand opening. But without a church in the making, even our best-laid, well-funded, and prayer-supported plans will fail. If God is truly building his church, then he is constantly cultivating new churches all around us. He does this by raising up leaders in a community and giving them spiritual parenthood over a group of people. When the church finally starts, it's more of a formality than a fresh beginning. It's a vision that doesn't need to be sold, but mobilized. Why we would ever abandon the work God has been doing through us, in order to initiate a new one, is beyond me.

This is not to say we should never go to hard-to-reach places. Many of us are called to be "parachute drop planters." But in this case we have to think like a missionary, or the pressure to produce organizational results will overtake us. We have to invest the same amount of time and effort in relationships as other planters, but our time starts now, so the season of harvest will come much later than everyone else's. It's a shame that church planters feel pressured to start services so quickly because, once we go public, we can never go back. It's too late to build a stronger core group; it's too late to cultivate our community; it's too late to expand our relational network; and it's too late to restore the sense of excitement and hope that only comes from new beginnings.

Starting a church in the making isn't just a sociological mandate; it's a spiritual one. If you look throughout Scripture, you'll find that God has always used social forces to propel his gospel. Church planting doesn't have to be as difficult as we've made it out to be. New churches can grow out of existing relationships. Church planters don't have to move to far away places to be considered faithful. And we don't have to wait and see if God will bless our efforts. He is already invested in the process. He cares much more than we do that new churches carry his gospel from generation to generation. Of course he doesn't want the process to be broken. So he gives us a church in the making.

God invites us to join him in advancing the kingdom. We don't have to start from scratch. We don't have to face impossible odds. We get to be a part of what he's been doing all along. Beneath the surface he has been building a tremendous root system that will yield a healthy, vibrant, and successful church. But we have to seize it. We have to identify it. So take up this great work. Cultivate good ground in your community; develop the social network around you; and plant your roots deep in a local community. You'll discover a natural, organic way of reproducing new congregations.